SELECTED SAYINGS FROM
PERFECTION OF WISDOM

The Prajñāpāramitā figure referred to on page 7

SELECTED SAYINGS

FROM THE

PERFECTION OF WISDOM

Chosen, arranged, and translated by

EDWARD CONZE

1978

PRAJÑĀ PRESS

Boulder

PRAJÑĀ PRESS
GREAT EASTERN BOOK COMPANY
P.O. BOX 271
BOULDER, COLORADO 80306

ⓒ1955 EDWARD CONZE
ISBN 0-87773-709-6

PUBLISHED BY ARRANGEMENT WITH
THE BUDDHIST SOCIETY
58 ECCLESTON SQUARE
LONDON SW1, ENGLAND

PRINTED IN THE UNITED STATES OF AMERICA

TABLE OF CONTENTS

FRONTISPIECE

A Prajnaparamita Rupa

THIS statue* of the four-armed Prajñāpāramitā, at present in the possession of Mr. and Mrs. Christmas Humphreys, was made in Nepal at a date not easy to determine. It is of solid bronze, and that by itself suggests an early date. Mr. Chintamoni Kar has assigned the statue to the ninth to tenth century, whereas I myself believe that the twelfth or thirteenth century is a safer guess.

The *two central hands* are in the gesture of teaching the Dharma. Of the extra arms, the right hand holds a *rosary* (which is missing here), and the left a *book*, which is understood to be a palm leaf manuscript of the Prajñāpāramitā. In many Buddhist countries a rosary is an essential part of the equipment of both monks and laymen. Western Buddhists have not yet sufficiently appreciated its significance, and they often believe that they can do without it. For meditation on the lines of the Prajñāpāramitā it is, however, quite indispensable. The actual rosary has 108 beads (the twelve signs of the zodiac multiplied by the nine planets), but for artistic reasons the one in the hands of the Prajñāpāramitā is usually restricted to sixteen, or more. The *third* eye is the "eye of wisdom" which, in the Sutra itself, has somewhat cryptically been defined as the vision by which one sees no dharma, knows no dharma, and discerns no dharma. Less paradoxically, the commentaries describe the "wisdom eye" as the ability to know the true character of reality. The *crown* indicates that the Prajñāpāramitā is to be regarded as an advanced Bodhisattva, who has reached the eighth Stage, and has won sovereignty over the world. The *seating position* is that most suitable to meditation and it is assumed that a person who has realised perfect wisdom does not leave the state of meditative trance while engaged in works on behalf of the welfare of living beings. These are the main points of iconographic interest.

From an artistic point of view this is one of the finest representations of Prajñāpāramitā I have ever seen. No photograph can do justice to it, and give us an idea of the delicacy of the

* See Frontispiece

features, rather South Indian in cast, and of the jewelled ornaments, of the soft sheen of the golden surface, or even of the symmetry and majesty of the proportions.

It may be useful to add two further observations about the background of this statue :

First, the design of cult images was not left to the arbitrary imagination of individual artists, but it was laid down strictly and once for all in documents called Sadhanas. The Sadhana which describes the four-armed Prajñāpāramitā has been translated by Dr. Snellgrove as No. 191 of *Buddhist Texts through the Ages*, and by reading it one comes to appreciate the yogic background of these figures. We have here, however, one of the few cases where the artistic execution differs from the rules. According to the Sadhana the second right arm, instead of holding a rosary, should be raised in the gesture which expresses the gift of confidence to others, and which can be seen for instance on the famous statue of the Buddha from Mathura. A concern for artistic symmetry must have induced the artists to generally depart from this prescription, which has been observed only in a few isolated instances on Lamaist block prints.

Secondly, Buddhist figures are rarely found alone, and almost invariably they form part of a group. The four-armed Prajñāpāramitā is often represented on manuscripts of the Pala period, and then she is surrounded by beautiful Tārās. As a statue she is normally a part of the famous Trinity which consists of the Buddha, Dharma and Samgha. Nepalese shrines often contain this Trinity with the Buddha in the centre, on his right the four-armed Prajñāpāramitā, representing Dharma, and on his left the four-armed Avalokitesvara, representing the Samgha. In these Trinities the construction of Avalokitesvara is closely analogous to that of the Prajñā-pāramitā, but he is male, the central hands are in the gesture of worship, and the extra left hand holds a lotus. By this symbolism the Mahayanists of Nepal, and also of other countries, wished to express the idea that the Prajñāpāramitā is the essence of the Dharma, and that the essential function of the Samgha is to act from a feeling of compassion for other beings. In all probability the statue I have here commented on formed part of such a Trinity, and it is helpful to remember this when one tries to understand its spiritual significance.

PREFACE

A NUMBER of these selections, approximately one-fifth of the total, have been previously printed in the Mahayana section of *Buddhist Texts through the Ages*, an Anthology which I edited in 1954. They could not be omitted here because otherwise the carefully planned balance of the readings would have been destroyed. In 1952, in the last issue of *Stepping Stones*, the Bhikshu Sangharakshita, of Kalimpong, began to print this collection of sayings from the Prajñāpāramitā. Funds soon gave out, and only the first instalment appeared. Now the Buddhist Society has taken over this venture, which began nine years ago in the pages of *The Middle Way* with two articles on "The scriptural background of the Hridaya Sutra". By way of Introduction I have added three articles from *The Middle Way* (1952-3)

The translator has been attracted to these writings from his early youth onwards, he has devoted twenty-five years of his life to their scholarly investigation, and he believes that he has done little violence to their letter. As to their spirit, who can say ?

October, 1954   EDWARD CONZE.

AUTHOR'S PREFACE TO THE THIRD EDITION

THIS book, one of the pioneer efforts of the Buddhist Society, has sold much more widely than anticipated at the time of its original publication. This is due partly to the rapid growth of interest in Zen, and partly to the fact that the message of the Prajñāpāramitā is so provocative, because it is at variance with everything in this age.

Over the last twenty-five years practically all the Prajñāpāramitā Texts have been translated into English. The short survey of the literature in the Introduction to this book was worked in 1960 into a full scale text book, *The Prajñāpāramitā Literature,* which has been so much in demand that a new up-to-date edition will soon be published in Tokyo. Thanks to Professor Lamotte, we have gained access, in French, to the first four volumes of Nāgārjuna's commentary on the Large Prajñāpāramitā Sūtra. These efforts of translating the Prajñāpāramitā literature have evoked great interest in the scholarly world in general. The Berkeley Buddhist Studies Series has brought out "Studies in Honor of Edward Conze" under the title of *Prajñāpāramitā and Related Systems,* edited by Lewis Lancaster. All in all, the humble publication of this volume ultimately has led to quite a success story. Let us hope in this case Dean Inge was wrong when he said, "In religion nothing fails as much as success."

June, 1978   EDWARD CONZE

INTRODUCTION

I. THE LITERATURE ON PERFECT WISDOM

THE literature on Perfect Wisdom, vast, deep and vital to an understanding of the Mahayana, has so far been rather neglected by Western students. The literary form of these texts is alien to European conventions, while their doctrine conflicts with the assumptions of practical men everywhere, and particularly with the habits of thought prevalent in this technical age. Nevertheless a few people here and there feel drawn to the complete unworldliness of this type of thought. They may welcome some more information about the relevant Indian literature.

A survey of the whole literature has never been attempted before, but a knowledge of the extent and development of these writings is obviously the first step towards their understanding. The enumeration of their titles makes dull reading, but is indispensable for reference. An infinitesimal part of this literature has so far been published in European languages. Even to a scholar it is not easily accessible. For much of it he must look in the huge oblong block prints of the Kanjur, the closely printed Chinese pages of the Taisho Issaikyo, or in Sanskrit manuscripts, often illegible and inaccurate, and scattered over the principal libraries of Europe and Asia.

The composition of Prajñāpāramitā texts extended over about 1,000 years. Roughly speaking, four phases can be distinguished : 1. The elaboration of a *basic text* (ca. 100 B.C. to A.D. 100), 2. The expansion of that text (ca. A.D. 100 to 300), 3. The re-statement of the doctrine in short Sutras and in *versified Summaries* ca. 300 to 500), and 4. The period of *Tantric* influence, and of the composition of *Commentaries* (ca. 500 to 1,200).

1. The oldest text is the *Perfection of Wisdom in 8,000 Lines*

---

[1] After each text I give in brackets the chief languages in which it can be read, i.e. S (anskrit), Ch(inese), T(ibetan), E(nglish), F(rench), and G(erman). I use capital letters where the whole text, small letters (s, ch, etc.) where only a part is available in that language. An Em indicates that the work forms part of my typed translation of the Prajñāpāramitā. (See the Advertisement at the end). In addition there are often other translations—into Mongol, Manchu, Khotanese, Japanese, etc., which I ignore here.

(S, Ch, T, f, g, Em)[1], in thirty-two chapters. Most of the Sutras of this Class, although in prose, are named after the number of Lines (shloka) which they contain, a shloka being thirty-two syllables. The English translation is about 110,000 words long. Some parts of this basic Prajñāpāramitā probably date back to 100 B.C. Other sections were added at later times, and the whole may have taken about two centuries to compose. This text is likely to have originated among the Mahāsanghikas, in the South, in the Andhra country, on the Kistna River near Amaravati. It claims to be the "second turning of the wheel of the Law", following on the preaching of the Hinayana. The doctrine of emptiness, in its many ramifications, is its main topic.

A verse summary of the original Prajñāpāramitā, or at least of its first twenty-eight chapters, is called *Verses on the Accumulation of the Precious Qualities of the Perfection of Wisdom* (S, Ch, T, Em), also in thirty-two chapters. Many of the earlier Mahayana Sutras exist in two forms, in verse and in prose. Usually the verse form is the earlier of the two. The original Ratnagunasamcayagāthā is now lost, and all we possess is Haribhadra's revision, which brings the text in line with the chapter divisions of the version in 8,000 Lines, as it existed in the eighth century. Chapters twenty-nine to thirty-two of this work form a new and additional treatise on the first five perfections.

2. About the beginning of the Christian era the basic Prajñāpāramitā was expanded into a "Large Prajñāpāramitā", as represented today by three different texts,—*Perfect Wisdom in 100,000 Lines* (S, Ch, T,) *Perfect Wisdom in 25,000 Lines* (Ch, T, e-m,) and *Perfect Wisdom in 18,000 Lines* (s, Ch, T). These three texts are really one and the same book. They only differ in the extent to which the "repetitions" are copied out : A great deal of traditional Buddhist meditation is a kind of repetitive drill, which applies certain laws or principles to a certain number of fixed categories. If, for instance, you take the statement the "X is emptiness, and the very emptiness is X", then the version in 100,000 Lines laboriously applies this principle to about 200 items, beginning with form, and ending with the dharmas, or attributes, which are characteristic of a Buddha. The versions in 25,000 and in 18,000 Lines are so much shorter because they give fewer items, sometimes only the first and the last. The Large Prajñāpāramitā falls into

three parts : The first third (Em) expands the first chapter of the version in 8,000 Lines. The second part reproduces, with some additions and omissions, the chapters two to twenty-eight of the same text. The third part is an independent treatise, which is throughout concerned with the obvious conflict between the doctrine of universal emptiness, and the practical needs of the struggle for enlightenment.

The first two centuries of the Christian era produced also a gigantic *Commentary* on the version in 25,000 Lines, which is traditionally ascribed to Nāgārjuna (ch, f). It contains a staggering wealth of useful information, and reflects the attitude of the Madhyamika School. From Nāgārjuna's circle also comes the beautiful *Hymn to Perfect Wisdom* (S, Ch, E, F), which is the work of *Rahulabhadra*.

In addition we have a *Perfect Wisdom in 10,000 Lines* (T). The first two chapters collect many of the definitions which are scattered through the Large Prajñāpāramitā. The remaining thirty chapters largely reproduce the version in 8,000 Lines. Two small texts, more in the nature of specialised treatises, probably belong to this period. The one, a *Perfect Wisdom in 500 Lines* (Ch, F, f), also called "The Questions of (the Bodhisattva) Nāgasrī", applies the basic concepts of the Prajñāpāramitā to the various aspects of begging for alms, of eating, of food, etc. The other, the *Prajñāpāramitā Sutra Explaining How Benevolent Kings may Protect their Countries* (Ch, e,) is mainly concerned with the practical effects of the Prajñāpāramitā on society. It explains how a ruler's devotion to the Prajñāpāramitā will increase his merit, and will call forth the protection of great and mighty Bodhisattvas, who will ward off all calamities from his country and its people. The greater part of this Sutra may have been written in China.

3. The huge bulk of the Large Prajñāpāramitā, a result of the creative exuberance of the Mahayana in its prime, proved an obstacle to later generations. Even men like Asanga "could no longer ascertain its meaning, because of the great number of the repetitions, their inability to distinguish the different words and arguments, and its profundity".[2] The challenge was met in two ways : By new, shorter Sutras, and by condensed Summaries of the large text.

Among the shorter Sutras, the finest are the two earliest,

[2] So Haribhadra, Abhisamayālankārāloka, p. 75.

both of the fourth century,—The *Heart Sutra* (S, Ch, T, E, F), in 25, or 14, and the *Diamond Sutra* (S, Ch, T, E, F, G), in 300 Lines. The "Heart Sutra", one of the sublimest spiritual documents of mankind, is a re-statement of the four Holy Truths, re-interpreted in the light of the dominant idea of emptiness.[3] The *Diamond Sutra*, in thirty-two short chapters, in spite of its apparently chaotic arrangement of great renown in the East, does not pretend to give a systematic survey of the teachings of the Prajñāpāramitā. It confines itself to a few central topics, and appeals directly to a spiritual intuition which has left the conventions of logic far behind.

Sutras of the same type, probably of the fifth and the early sixth century, are the *Perfect Wisdom in 700 Lines* (S, Ch, T, Em) the *Perfect Wisdom in 2,500 Lines* (S, Ch, T, em), also known as the "Questions of Suvikrāntavikrāmin", and a rather un-distinguished *Perfect Wisdom in 50 Lines* (Ch, T, Em). The version in 700 Lines deserves to be better known. It tries to accord a novel treatment to all the basic teachings of Perfect Wisdom. From the earlier works it differs by its stress on the startling, paradoxical, self-contradictory and nonsensical character of the doctrine of emptiness. Another new feature, observed also in the "Questions of Suvikrāntavikrāmin", is the endeavour to bring out the "hidden meaning" of the sayings of the Buddha. Here we may see the influençe of the Yogā-cārins.

Among the *Summaries* the most outstanding is the *Abhisamayālankāra*[1] (S, T, E), also a work of the fourth century. Its authorship is uncertain. Perhaps it may be ascribed to the Madhyamika-Yogacarin *Maitreyanātha*, a teacher of Asanga. The work is a brilliant versified Table of Contents, in 273 memorial verses, to the Prajñāpāramitā in 25,000 Lines, and at the same time it assigns to each section of the text a place on the stages of spiritual progress which Buddhist tradition has mapped out, thus everywhere showing the practical way by which one can become a Buddha. Although too schematic at times, this work is invaluable for anyone who wishes to study the Sutra. In both India and Tibet it has dominated the exegesis of the Large Prajñāpāramitā for centuries to come,

---

[3] For the detailed proof see the *Journal of the Royal Asiatic Society 1948*, pp. 33-51.

[1] "Treatise on the re-union (with the Absolute)"

whereas in China it has apparently remained unknown. The divisions of the Abhisamayālankāra were at some later time, probably in the fifth or sixth century, inserted into the text of one of the recensions of the version in 25,000 Lines. This work exists in Sanskrit, Tibetan and Mongol. Other Yogā-cārins also wrote versified Summaries of the teachings of the Prajñāpāramitā, *Asanga* in the form of a Shastra to the "Diamond Sutra" (S, Ch), and *Dignaga* (ca. 450) in his *Pindārtha* (S, Ch, T, E), which arranges the teachings under thirty-two subjects, and dwells chiefly on the sixteen kinds of emptiness and the antidotes to the ten kinds of false imputation.

4. A further condensation of the Prajñāpāramitā was, of course, possible. It could be compressed into the short, but effective, form of spells,—either Mantras or Dharanis. This step was taken already in the fourth century, and in the "Heart Sutra" we find a Mantra of the Prajñāpāramitā. Under the influence of Tantric modes of thought a number of Tantric abbreviations of the Prajñāpāramitā, all very short, were composed between 600 and 1,200. The most interesting is the *Perfection of Wisdom in a Few Words* (S, Ch, T, Em), which is designed as a counterpart to the "Heart Sutra". While the "Heart Sutra" is addressed to the spiritual élite, this Sutra appeals to the less endowed, to beings who have "but little capacity to act", who "have little merit". who are "dull and stupified". Nine other Tantric Prajñāpāramitā Sutras are found in the Tibetan collection of the Scriptures. One of them, *Perfect Wisdom in One Letter* (T, Em), deserves mention for its brevity, the one letter A being said to contain and represent the Perfection of Wisdom. Another text gives the *108 Names* (*or epithets*) *of Perfect Wisdom* (T, Em), and another the *25 Doors* by which Perfect Wisdom can be approached (T, Em)[2].

A Tantric text which is in a class by itself is the *Perfection of Wisdom in 150 Lines* (S, Ch, T, Em). The ten works mentioned above express the traditional ideas of the older Prajñā-pāramitā works, and only the mode of expressing them is Tantric, employing mythological concepts, mantras, etc. This text, on the other hand, although called a Prajñāpāramitā, expounds the new ideas of Tantric Buddhism. It consists of

---

[2] For the sake of completeness I give the titles of the remaining texts : There is a Perfection of Wisdom for Kausika (S, Ch, T, Em), for Suryagarbha (T, Em), Candragarbha (T, Em), Samantabhadra (T, Em), Vajrapani (T, Em) and Vaj-raketu (T, Em). In addition several Prajñāpāramitā Dharanis (S) are known.

a series of fourteen short litanies, followed by a poem, and uses the new esoteric terminology of the Tantra, abounding in such words as vajra (thunderbolt), guhya (mystery), siddhi (magical success), krodha (wrath), etc.

Finally, personified as a deity, the Perfection of Wisdom becomes the object of a cult, and a number of *Ritual Texts* describe the methods by which her spiritual power can be evoked. *The Sādhanamālā* (S, T), has preserved nine Sadhanas, or devices for conjuring up, various, iconographically distinct, forms of the Prajñāpāramitā. Five more Ritual Texts, translated between 600 and 1,000, are preserved in Chinese.

Indian literary tradition regards a sacred text as incomplete without a *Commentary*. The Prajñāpāramitā is no exception, and the majority of its versions have found a commentator. The work of interpretation went on steadily from the fifth century onwards, and increased in momentum under the Pala dynasty which, between 750 and 1,200, ruled over Magadha and Bengal, and patronised a Buddhism which combined Prajñāpāramitā and Tantra. About twenty Pala commentaries are still extant, mostly in Tibetan translation. The most important, the work of *Haribhadra* (ca. A.D. 770) combines a commentary on the version in 8,000 Lines with an explanation of the Abhisamayālankāra.

After 1,200 there are no more works on Prajñāpāramitā in India. In India the tradition itself was absorbed and carried on by the Vedānta. In China, Japan and Tibet the Prajñāpāramitā remained the basis of all Mahayana teaching, and in those lands it has borne wonderful fruit. Among its later developments the flowering of Zen is not the least noteworthy.

II. THE TEACHINGS OF PRAJNAPARAMITA

The teachings of the Prajñāpāramitā have little significance for the present age. To be quite truthful, they are equally irrelevant to any other age. They are meant for people who have withdrawn from society, and who have little, if any, interest in its problems. They were addressed either to monks, or to pious householders who, though in the world, were not of it, intent on becoming monks, if not here then in a later life. Leaving worldlings to get on with their worldly problems, these Sutras assume that the whole sense-linked, or conditioned, world is unsatisfactory, and that preoccupation with it is unworthy of our true mission in life. To make anything of them, one must take this for granted, and they do not elaborate the point any further. In addition, one must be fairly familiar with the Tripitaka, for its sayings are all the time in the background of the discussion. In particular, one should be acquainted with the terminology of the Abhidharma, and with its methods and the results that can be expected from their more or less prolonged practice. The Prajñāpāramitā is by no means an elementary text, which could be grasped apart from the traditions which lead up to it. For our efforts to sever the bonds which tie us to this conditioned world we have at our disposal practices which train either the will, or the emotions, or the intellect. The potential adept of the Prajñāpāramitā will be a person with a marked preference for the intellectual methods, with a strong urge to penetrate to the real being of things by cognitive means, with a strong inclination to metaphysical thinking. As a Temperance movement would give no sense without the widespread desire to drink to excess, so only intellectual people would have a motive to battle hard against the falsifications of the intellect, and to baffle, exhaust and defeat it.

We must further assume that a Buddhist has trained himself for some time in the prescribed traditional methods, and has gained a fair measure of detachment from the things of the world. No longer hopelessly tied to the pursuit of wealth, power, sex, social position, or whatever it may be, not unduly weighed down by possessions, not unduly consumed by envy or desire for fame, not unduly stifled by neurotic self-absorption, he has recollected his old spiritual home, and tries his wings to fly back to it. Spiritual progress will then be marked by a reorganisation of all his motives and interests. Whereas, before, a man was dominated by his five senses, his conduct is now increasingly guided by faith, vigour, mindfulness, concentration and wisdom. And the growth of these five virtues must lead to the emergence of a variety of spiritual attainments. At the same time a longing for the Absolute makes itself felt, and attention shifts more and more towards that which is not of this world, towards the Unconditioned, which does not share in the faults of the conditioned. "There is something which is Unborn, Unbecome, Unmade, Unconditioned, and without

B

it there would be no escape from these things which are born, which become, which are made and conditioned". Now, once a man has reached the Absolute, the Prajñāpāramitā will be of little use to him. "This discourse on Dharma is like a raft", which is discarded once one has reached the other shore. But for a while, after one has got the Absolute into view, and while one is in the process of moving towards it, these texts may help a great deal.

The reason is not far to seek. The very means and objects of emancipation are apt to turn into new objects and channels of craving. Attainments may harden into personal possessions; spiritual victories and achievements may increase one's self-conceit ; merit is hoarded as a treasure in heaven which no one can take away ; enlightenment and the Absolute are misconstrued as things out there to be gained. In other words, the old vicious trends continue to operate in the new spiritual medium. The Prajñāpāramitā is designed as the antidote to the more subtle forms of self-seeking which replace the coarser forms after the spiritual life has grown to some strength and maturity.

The problem is fundamental and unavoidable. Strictly speaking, any position adopted towards Nirvana is an impossible one. Any attitude to it is bound to be self-contradictory. Nirvana, as the extinction of all desire, cannot itself be an object of desire. If one wishes for it, and one must necessarily do so while on the way to it, one mistakes it for what it is not. Its traditional attributes remind us that, taken as such, it is quite unattractive. Nirvana is called the Signless, because it cannot be recognised for what it is ; the Wishless, because it cannot be desired ; the Void, because it does not concern us at all.

So much about the *public* for which the Prajñāpāramitā Sutras are intended, and the *problem* which they set out to solve. What then is their *subject matter* ? It is just the Unconditioned, nothing but the Absolute, over and over again. On the face of it there could be nothing more dreary and uninteresting than the "Unconditioned,"—a grey patch, a wan abstraction, an elusive will-o'-the-wisp. But it is a fact of observation that in the course of their spiritual struggle people come to a stage where this abstraction miraculously comes to life, gains a body, fills and irradiates the soul. It is then that the Prajñāpāramitā acquires its interest and meanings. Out of the abundance of the heart the mouth speaketh. The lengthy writings on Perfect Wisdom are one long declamation in praise of the Absolute. So much is, of course, generally known about the Absolute, that nothing can usefully be said about it. Faced with this fact, the Old Wisdom School kept silent, or at least nearly silent about it. The Prajñāpāramitā, on the other hand, considers everything that *might* reasonably be said about it, and expressly rejects it as untrue or inadequate. In any case it observes the precaution of always cancelling out each statement by another one which contradicts it. Everywhere in these writings contradiction is piled upon contradiction. Whatever is said about the Absolute gives really no sense, but, on occasions, people feel the mental need to say it. What we think and say about people we love is, strictly speaking, never quite true. But it would be unnatural not to say or think it. So with the Absolute. The Prajñāpāramitā expresses a state of intoxication with the Unconditioned, and at the same time it attempts to cope with it, and to sober it down.

III. THE DOCTRINE OF EMPTINESS

What then are the *positive teachings* of the writings on Prajñāpāramitā ? A bald summary can do no justice to them, and if their authors had thought it possible to expound them in two thousand words, they would not have used hundreds of thousands. Briefly, the teaching concerns the relation between conditioned and unconditioned things. Something is called "conditioned" if it is what it is only in relation to something else. All the familiar things of our everyday world are conditioned in two ways : Each one is dependent on a multiplicity of other events which surround it, and all of them are linked to suffering and ignorance through the twelve links of the chain of causation (or, more literally, of "conditioned co-production"). The "Diamond Sutra" concludes with the famous verse (No. 84) :

> "As stars, a fault of vision, as a lamp,
> A mock show, dew drops, or a bubble,
> A dream, a lightning flash, or cloud,
> So we should view what is conditioned".

Like *dew drops* and a *lightning flash* the things of this world are evanescent and short-lived. Each experience bursts soon, like a *bubble*, and it can be enjoyed only for a moment. The transformations of the earthly scene concern us, and our true welfare, no more than the changing shapes of the *clouds* we may watch on a hot summer day. The appearance of this world is like a *hallucination* which springs from a disease in the organ of vision—about as real as the spots which livery people see before their eyes. Like a *magical show* it deceives, deludes and defrauds us, and it is false, when measured by what we slowly learn about ultimate reality. As a *lamp* goes on burning only as long as fuel is fed into it, so also this world of ours continues only while craving supplies the drive. The enlightened awake to reality as it is ; compared with their vision of true reality our normal experience is that of a *dream*, unreal and not to be taken seriously. Finally, what we see around us can be likened to the *stars*. As the stars are no longer seen when the sun has risen, so also the things of this world are visible only in the darkness of ignorance, and, in the absence of the normal mental reactions to them, they are no longer noticed when the true non-dual gnosis of the Absolute has taken place.

So far, in this delineation of the attributes of the conditioned, there is nothing in the teachings of the Prajñāpāramitā that is not also found in the Tipitaka or in Buddhaghosa. We do, however, come across a new departure when we read that "a fully enlightened Buddha is like a magical illusion, is like a dream", and so is Nirvana, and "even if perchance there could be anything more distinguished than Nirvana, even that is like an illusion, like a dream". (No. 86). The conditioned is here equated with the unconditioned. And that unconditioned identity of the conditioned and of the Unconditioned is the principal message of the Prajñāpāramitā.

This quite incomprehensible Absolute is perpetually held before us as a standard. With it we should identify, into it we should sink ourselves. We are, indeed, taught to view the world as it appears when the individual self is extinct. All hidden concern for self-advancement is counteracted. One should not aim at a private and personal Nirvana, which would exclude others and the world, but at the full omniscience of a Buddha which somehow includes both (No. 5-6). Personal merit must be surrendered to all beings (No. 15-17). No personal attainment is, in any case, possible, (No. 70-71), no entity can provide lasting rest and security, no freedom is complete while constrained by the need to keep anything out. In every way the Prajñāpāramitā attempts to correct misconceptions which the practices of the Abhidharma may have fostered. The Abhidharma had convinced us that there are no "beings" or "persons", but only bundles of dharmas. Yet, although beings are not there, they must nevertheless, from compassion, not be abandoned, and their welfare, though strictly non-existent, must be furthered by "skill in means". The Abhidharma had rejected all conditioned things as perilous. Now one realises the peril of keeping them apart from the Unconditioned. The Abhidharma had cultivated wisdom as the virtue which permits one to see the "own being" of dharmas. Now the *perfection* of wisdom in its turn regards the separateness of these dharmas as merely a provisional construction, and it is cultivated as the virtue which permits us to see everywhere just one emptiness. All forms of multiplicity are condemned as the arch enemies of the higher spiritual vision and insight. When duality is hunted out of all its hiding places, the results are bound to be surprising. Not only are the multiple objects of thought identified with one mysterious emptiness, but the very instruments of thought take on a radically new character when affirmation and negation are treated as non-different, as one and the same. Once we jump out of our intellectual habits, emptiness is revealed as the concrete fullness ; no longer remote, but quite near ; no longer a dead nothingness beyond, but the life-giving womb of the Buddha within us.

This doctrine of emptiness has baffled more than one enquirer, and one must indeed despair of explaining it if it is treated as a mere theoretical proposition, on a level with other theoretical statements. And yet, everything is really quite simple, as soon as one pays attention to the spiritual intention behind this doctrine. In teaching "emptiness" the Prajñāpāramitā does not propound the view that only the Void exists. The bare statement that "everything is really emptiness" is quite meaningless. It is even false, because the rules of this particular logic demand that the emptiness must be as well denied as affirmed. Among its eighteen kinds of emptiness, the large Sutra on Perfect Wisdom distinguishes as the fourth the "emptiness of emptiness", which is defined by saying that "the emptiness of all dharmas is empty of that emptiness".

In its function, shunyata, or emptiness, has been likened to salt. It should pervade the religious life, and give flavour to it, as salt does with food. By itself, eaten in lumps, salt is not particularly palatable, and neither is "emptiness". When one insists on emptiness one aims at revealing the Infinite by removing that which obscures it. One denies the finite, one-sided, partial nature of affirmative propositions, not in order to then replace them by just another affirmative proposition, but with an eye to transcending and eliminating all affirmation, which is but a hidden form of self-assertion. The Void is brought in not for its own sake, but as a method which leads to the penetration into true reality. It opens the way to a direct approach to the true nature of things (dharmatā) by removing all adherence to words which abstract from reality instead of disclosing it.

We shall never get anywhere with this concept of emptiness, unless we treat it as what it is, as a guide to meditation. Without further ado, I will therefore now set out the five stages of the meditation on emptiness, as the tradition of the Prajñā-pāramitā reveals it.

(1) For a beginning one must attend to the *emptiness of dharmas*. In order to do that, one must first of all understand what a dharma is, as distinct from a thing or a person, must learn the Abhidharma teachings in their many details, and acquire some skill in reviewing everyday experiences in terms of dharmas. If one fails to take this preliminary step, one will never get any further in this quest for emptiness, because one fails to develop even the foundations of the subjective counterpart of emptiness, which is "wisdom". Here I must take this for granted, and can only point out that, by taking the trouble to become acquainted with the tradition on dharmas, one has already taken the first step towards emptiness. For these dharmas are "empty" in the sense that in this world of dharmic fact no real entity corresponds to such words as "self", "I", "mine", or to their derivatives, such as soul, substance, property, belonging, owning, person, etc. Dharmas are void of self.

(2) One next makes the distinction between conditioned and unconditioned dharmas, to which I have referred above. On the second stage one attends to those features of all *conditioned dharmas* which distinguish them from the unconditioned. One then has to learn that we are normally in the habit of

attributing features to conditioned dharmas which are actually exclusively found in the Absolute, and that we habitually overrate the degree of permanence, happiness and ownership which are found in conjunction with them. One also gets on this stage a clearer notion of one's own true spiritual nature, and feels that our spiritual side can be satisfied with nothing less than eternity, unmixed bliss and omnipotence. The unconditioned is here used as a standard by which the conditioned is measured, and found wanting. If one persists in these meditations for some length of time, one will clearly see that all conditioned dharmas are "empty" in the sense that they lack a true self, lack anything that is worth being called a "self". Only that which has complete self-control would be worth being called a "self". No conditioned event can have anything like it, and therefore and in that sense it is void, and unworthy of being regarded as a reliable point of attachment, as a refuge or support, as a home or a source of security.

(3) When one feels that all conditioned events are not worth having, that they should all be forsaken, one can attend to Nirvana, the *Unconditioned*. This, in its turn, is again called "emptiness", for two reasons : Because it is the freedom from any identification with anything conditioned, and because it does not concern us, as individuals. Our individual self and its identifications are outside it. It is void of them.

(4) It is only after one has undergone these three progressive stages of meditation that one can move on from wisdom to perfect wisdom, and that one reaches the threshold of the emptiness with which the Sutras on the Perfection of Wisdom are concerned. The last two stages were based on the distinction and contrast between the conditioned and the unconditioned. It is now necessary to again undo that distinction, and to contemplate the *identity of the world and of Nirvana*, with the aim of transcending both their identity and their difference. One now regards emptiness as the identity of yes and no, and therewith a vast realm of paradoxes opens before us. All things are unborn, but even when born they remain undistinguished from the original Void. All things are inactive, but even self-active exertion is not different from the peaceful calm of Nirvana. As the identity of subject and object this emptiness is Suchness, beyond all possibilities of misconception, beyond all categories of thought. It is beyond all possibility of

attainment,—by body, word, or thought,—and yet it saves all.

(5) But even this approach has to be transcended again. The paradoxes are finally left behind, and one comes to a stage of *silence*, where nothing at all can be said.

The "Heart Sutra" (No. 54) has these five stages in view when it ends with the formula : "Gone, gone, gone beyond, gone altogether beyond, O what an awakening, All Hail !" "Gone", from the data of common sense to the dharmas, and their emptiness. "Gone", from infatuation with conditioned dharmas to their renunication, because of their emptiness. "Gone beyond", to the Unconditioned, and to its emptiness. "Gone altogether beyond", even beyond the difference between the world and Nirvana, to a transcendent non-duality, in which affirmation and negation are identified in one emptiness. "O what an awakening", the final stage of transcendental emptiness, in which the long sleep is at last over. It will be seen that the word "emptiness" in each case derives its meaning from the context created by a spiritual attitude. Outside that context it has no meaning at all.

To repeat once more : Emptiness is not a theory, but a ladder that reaches out into the infinite. A ladder is not there to be discussed, but to be climbed. If one does not even take the first steps on it, the farther rungs seem, I admit, rather remote. They come nearer only as one goes up there. "Emptiness" is used as a traditional term to express the complete negation of this world by the exercise of wisdom. The central idea is the total denial of, the complete emancipation from, the world around us in all its aspects and along its entire breadth. It is a practical concept, and it embodies an aspiration, not a view. Its only use is to help us to get rid of this world and of the ignorance which binds us to it. It has not only one meaning, but several, which can unfold themselves on the successive stages of the actual process of transcending the world through wisdom. Not everyone, of course, is meant to understand what emptiness means. In that case it is better to pass on to something else.

SELECTED SAYINGS FROM THE
PERFECTION OF WISDOM

FOREWORD

ROUGHLY forty Prajñāpāramitā Sutras have been composed in India over a period of a millenium, from 400 to 1,400 years after the Buddha's Nirvana, or between 100 B.C. and A.D. 900. The texts vary greatly in length, but their total bulk is considerable. They are in the form of dialogues between Buddhas, Bodhisattvas, and Disciples, and the language used is Sanskrit.

In this Anthology, the passages from the Sutras have been distributed under three main headings, according to whether they deal with the Buddha, the Dharma, or the Samgha. The usual order has, however, been inverted, and the Samgha comes first, and the Buddha last. The average reader is more likely in his spiritual development to be nearer to the condition of an ordinary member of the Samgha than to the perfection of a Buddha. The sayings which concern the Buddha are therefore among the most unintelligible in these Sutras, and if they were placed at the beginning of the book, few would trouble to read on. The teachings dealing with the Samgha, on the other hand, are fairly easy to grasp, and even full of human interest. It is in accordance with the elementary rules of "skill in means" that one should arrange the selections in a progressive order of difficulty, and this may explain the otherwise rather startling inversion of the order of the "Three Treasures".

I have tried to cover the whole ground, and no important aspect of the teaching has been omitted. Generally, in order to preserve the rhythm of the thought, I have preferred longer extracts to brief snippets. The more readable passages have been preferred everywhere, and technicalities have been avoided. Usually the translation is quite literal. On occasions, however, I have made slight stylistic alterations to ensure greater readability, and sometimes I have inserted in brackets short explanations from the commentaries. The reader will find that the more advanced tenets of the doctrine are often phrased in a strangely elusive and mystifying way. That is the intention of the Sutra itself, and it was the translator's duty to respect it.

A. THE SAMGHA

I. THE WORTHY AUDIENCE

*The Wisdom Sutras set out to describe, as far as it is possible,
the highest achievement of which man is capable. They pre-
suppose great self-denial, a pure spirituality, and a long practice
in meditation. We begin our extracts with some passages which
describe the type of person who is addressed in these Sutras,
and for whom they have relevance.*

1.

Suvikrāntavikrāmin : We do not question the Tathagata for
the sake of beings of inferior resolve, nor for those who have
weak hearts or poor minds, who are lazy or overcome by sloth,
who have sunk into the mud of false views, who are caught in
Mara's snare, who discredit the doctrine by their deeds, who
dread austerities, who are confused and not mindful, bewildered
in their hearts, or immersed in the dirt of sensuous pleasures,
who are dishonest and deceitful, or without gratitude, who
desire evil and habitually do it, whose morality has gone wrong,
whose morality is not perfectly pure, whose views have gone
wrong, who course in Mara's range, who exalt themselves
and deprecate others, who attach weight to gain and honour,
or are bent on food and robes,—cheats, chatterers, stargazers,
charlatans, keen on making a profit. We do not question the
Tathagata for the sake of beings of that kind.

But we question him for the sake of beings who strive after
the cognition of the all-knowing, the non-attached cognition,
the cognition of the Self-Existent, the unequalled cognition,
the utmost cognition ; for the sake of Bodhisattvas, of great
beings, who cannot exalt themselves nor deprecate others
because they apprehend neither themselves nor others, who have
slain all pride, who are like bulls with their horns sawn off,
Bodhisattvas whose stings are removed, lowly in mind, with the
hearts of young outcasts, or like the earth, or water, fire,
air or space. Not even Dharma do they apprehend, how much
less what is wrong (*a-dharma*). They do not settle down even
in Dharma, how much less in what is not the Dharma. Their
resolutions are pure, they are free from dishonesty and deceit,

upright, evenminded in their hearts, full of pity for all beings and desirous of their welfare. They instigate others to good actions, encite and encourage them. They carry the great burden, have mounted on the great vehicle, live for the great task, possess the great compassion, and bring benefits and happiness to all beings, as their guides, conductors, and leaders. They dwell unsupported by all dharmas, do not care for any of the objects in any of the sense-fields, or for any of the places of rebirth, they have escaped all the snares of Mara, are zealous, vigorous and vigilant, attain to the highest perfection in all dharmas, and have great skill in removing all kinds of uncertainty. For the sake of such beings, O Lord, of Bodhisattvas, of great beings, do we question the Tathagata. For the sake of those who put their minds not even to the cognition of a Buddha, do not settle down to it, do not adopt any inclination for it, who have completely transcended all mindings, are established on the Path, have progressed along it and point it out to others.

We question the Tathagata in the interest of the welfare of all beings, for their benefit, happiness and security, bearing in mind of all beings the happiness, the utmost happiness, the supreme happiness, the happiness of Nirvana, the happiness of the Buddha, the unconditioned happiness. We therefore question the Tathagata in order to remove the uncertainties of all beings. We ourselves, O Lord, want to be freed from uncertainty, and then, freed from uncertainty, we want to demonstrate the Dharma to all beings, so that they also might lose their uncertainties. For all beings, O Lord, want happiness and are averse to suffering. All beings are desirous of happiness but outside wisdom we do not see, O Lord, any happiness for any being. Apart from the mode of life adopted by Bodhisattvas there is nowhere any happiness for any being.

2.

Sariputra : But it is not for the sake of conceited people that this demonstration of Dharma takes place. There is no room here for the conceited, or for those who still struggle to forsake conceit. Conceit implies a claim to superiority. The conceited impute superiority to some things over others, and they do not see things as equal. Even those who see all things as equal remain uncertain about this Dharma. Only those who do not apprehend anything as equal or unequal, do not put their minds to anything as equal or unequal, and who therefore do not settle down in anything as equal or unequal,—only those will never be afraid of anything. There is no route here for all the foolish common people, and it lies outside their sphere. There is no route here either for those who belong to the vehicle of the Disciples, or for those who, belonging to the vehicle of the Pratyekabuddhas, course in deep dharmas. In these stainless dharmas there is no route either for those who belong to the vehicle of the Bodhisattvas, but who nevertheless course in a sign, who have not been taken hold of by the good friend, and who are in the hands of a bad teacher. They lie outside their sphere. We must, however, make an exception for those who belong to the vehicle of the Disciples, but have seen the Truth, are supported by the good friend, are resolved on deep dharmas and course in agreement with these dharmas, plunge and enter into these dharmas. But no stupefaction or hesitation is felt towards these dharmas by those Bodhisattvas who have left all signs behind and who course in the signless, who make no distinctions, who have just absolutely gone forth into deep dharmas, and who, whenever they may thus apprehend a thought, do not differentiate any dharma whatever, do not review it, and do not differentiate enlightenment as a separate entity. For they are established in agreement with all dharmas, and they are not in disagreement with them. Whenever they are asked about dharmas, in each case they reply in agreement with just the facts about them, and explain them in agreement with them.

The Lord : So it is, Ananda, as Sariputra explains. The conceited can find no ground to stand on in this demonstration of Dharma. For it is outside their sphere to enter into this enlightenment of a Buddha. In agreement with reality is this enlightenment of a Buddha. For the thought of beings of inferior resolve does not stride in sublime dharmas, in Buddhadharmas. For those who are of inferior resolve, and conceited, abide in a condition which is contrary to the enlightenment of a Buddha. They march along under the sway of conceit, and they cannot understand the deep Dharma. Pure is this assembly,—they have done their duties under the Jinas of the past, they have planted wholesome roots, they have honoured many Buddhas, they are resolved on deep dharmas, they have coursed in deep dharmas . . . A universal monarch might summon his many sons, all of good birth and pure race, and share out his vast store of treasures equally with all of them. He would give equally to all, and not one would he pass over. The sons will then feel a surpassing affection for the universal monarch, and a serene trust in him. They all feel that to him they are equally important. Just so the Tathagata, the king of Dharma, the master of Dharma, the Self-Existent, assembles these his sons, shares out to them the treasures of Dharma, and not one he passes over. Their affection, trust and respect for me grows steadily, and, as they all prevent an interruption of the lineage of the Buddhas, they are all equally important to me. But to other beings this treasure of Dharma means nothing,— to those who are of inferior resolve and conceited, who course in false views, who take the data of experience for signs of realities, who assume a basis somewhere, who are hit by the pride which thinks "I am", who are overcome by greed, hate and delusion, and who have strayed on to a wrong road. Beings of inferior resolve, unlike the sons of a universal monarch can, of course, find no pleasure in the wealth of a universal monarch. What could beggarly beings do with such sublime treasures ? Even if they could get them, they would not be glad, would not know what to do with them, and would either sell them cheaply or lose them through carelessness. For they are not conversant with precious things, and do not recognize them when they meet them. Even so the sons of the Tathagata, the Bodhisattvas, who have seen the Truth and who are great beings, certainly have an interest in this store of precious dharmas. This precious Dharma, associated as it is with the emptiness of non-apprehension, and with dharmas of a Buddha, pleases them well and seems good to them, and their business lies with it. What could beggarly beings do with this store of precious dharmas, beings destitute of learning, or confused by their learning, beings who are but blind fools ? Even if they have got it, they are bound to lose it again, or thoughtlessly part with it. For no outcast, nor refuse worker, no juggler, or any other being who lives like a beggar, can derive enjoyment from sublimely precious things, and will either sell them cheaply, or lose them. The heretics of other sects correspond to those "beggarly beings",—and that includes also the Disciples. All the foolish common people are "beggarly beings", all those who have sunk into the mud of false views, who lean on a basis, who are inclined to dullness, who treat the data of experience as signs of realities, who have strayed on to a wrong path. Certainly they cannot enjoy this precious Dharma. When they have got it, they are bound to lose it again, or part with it thoughtlessly. But the sons of the Buddha, who course in the range of the Buddhas, and who exist so that the lineage of the Tathagatas should not be interrupted,—when they gain this precious Dharma, they know how to enjoy and use it, they do not lose it again, they perceive its great value. A jackal does not enjoy the lion's roar. But the whelps of the lion, the offspring of the great lion, they enjoy his roar. Even so, like jackals, all the foolish common people, with their wrong views, are incapable of enjoying the great lion's roar of the Tathagata, nor can they enjoy or use the wealth of the great lion, the fully enlightened Buddha. But those who are the whelps of the fully enlightened Buddha, the offspring of the great lion, the Buddha, produced by him with the cognition of the Self-Existent,—they enjoy the roar of the great lion, of the fully enlightened Buddha, and they will do so for ever.

3.

The Lord : Unthinkable and incomparable, O Subhuti, is this discourse on Dharma. It has been taught by the Tathagata for the weal of beings who have set out in the best vehicle, for the weal of those who have set out in the most excellent vehicle. Those who will take up this discourse on Dharma, bear it in mind, recite it, study and illuminate it in full detail for others, they have been known, O Subhuti, by the Tathagata with his Buddha-cognition, they have been seen, O Subhuti, by the Tathagata with his Buddha-eye, they have been fully known to the Tathagata. All these beings, O Subhuti, will be blest with an infinite heap of merit, they will be blest with a heap of merit unthinkable, incomparable, measureless and unlimited. They will all have an equal share in enlightenment when they bear in mind, recite and assimilate this text. For it is not possible, O Subhuti, that this discourse of Dharma could be learned by beings of inferior resolve, or by such as have a self in view, or a being, or a soul, or a person. Nor can beings who have not taken the pledge of Bodhisattvas either learn this discourse on Dharma, or take it up, bear it in mind, recite or study it.

4.

The Lord : Who will believe when the exposition of the cognition of the Tathagata is thus expounded ?

Mañjusri : Those who will understand the meaning of this teaching are people who are not doomed to birth-and-death, nor are they, doomed to Parinirvana, set free. They are not shaken by their individuality, and yet their greed, hatred and delusion are not extinct. For non-extinction does not become extinct, nor go to complete extinction. Not having transcended birth-and-death, they are reckoned among birth-and-death. Not lacking in the Path, they do not produce a notion of the Path.

II. COMPASSION AND SKILL IN MEANS

The "perfection of wisdom" combines the contemplation of emptiness, by wisdom, with an active concern for the welfare of all living beings, which is based on compassion, and employs a great variety of devices, technically known as "skill in means".

1. THE SHORTCOMINGS OF THE DISCIPLES

Historically, the writings on perfect wisdom sprang from a discontent with the rather narrow interpretation of the doctrine which we now call "Hinayana", but which at that time was attributed to the "Disciples" of the Buddha, like Sariputra, and others. The "Disciples" train themselves for the purpose of becoming "Arhats", and they are often coupled with the "Pratyekabuddhas", who aim at the enlightenment of a Buddha, but refrain from preaching the doctrine after they have won enlightenment. The "selfishness" of Disciples and Pratyekabuddhas is frequently criticised in the Sutras on " perfect wisdom".

5.

The Lord : A Bodhisattva should not train in the same way in which persons belonging to the vehicle of the Disciples and Pratyekabuddhas are trained. How then are the Disciples and Pratyekabuddhas trained ? They make up their minds that "one single self we shall tame, one single self we shall pacify, one single self we shall lead to final Nirvana". Thus they undertake exercises which are intended to bring about wholesome roots for the sake of taming themselves, pacifying themselves, leading themselves to Nirvana. A Bodhisattva should certainly not in such a way train himself. On the contrary, he should train himself thus : "My own self I will place into Suchness, and, so that all the world might be helped, I will also place all beings into Suchness, and I will lead to Nirvana the whole immeasurable world of beings". With that intention should a Bodhisattva undertake all the exercises which further the spiritual progress of the world. But he should not boast about them.

6.

The Lord : What do you think, Sariputra, does it occur to any of the Disciples and Pratyekabuddhas to think that "after we have known full enlightenment, we should lead all beings to Nirvana, into the realm of Nirvana which leaves nothing behind " ?

Sariputra : No indeed, O Lord.

The Lord : One should therefore know that this wisdom of the Disciples and Pratyekabuddhas bears no comparison to the wisdom of a Bodhisattva. What do you think, Sariputra, does it occur to any of the Disciples and Pratyekabuddhas that "after I have practised the six perfections, have brought beings to maturity, have purified the Buddha-field, have fully gained the ten powers of a Tathagata, his four grounds of self-confidence, the four analytical knowledges and the eighteen special dharmas of a Buddha, after I have known full enlightenment, I shall lead countless beings to Nirvana "?

Sariputra : No, O Lord.

The Lord : But such are the intentions of a Bodhisattva. A glow-worm, or some other luminous animal, does not think that its light could illuminate the Continent of Jambudvipa, or radiate over it. Just so the Disciples and Pratyekabuddhas do not think that they should, after winning full enlightenment, lead all beings to Nirvana. But the sun, when it has risen, radiates its light over the whole of Jambudvipa. Just so a Bodhisattva, after he has accomplished the practices which lead to the full enlightenment of Buddhahood, leads countless beings to Nirvana.

7.

The Lord : Suppose, Subhuti, that there were a most excellent hero, very vigorous, of high social position, handsome, attractive and most fair to behold, of many virtues, in possession of all the finest virtues, of those virtues which spring from the very height of sovereignty, morality, learning, renunciation and so on. He is judicious, able to express himself, to formulate his views clearly, to substantiate his claims ; one who always knows the suitable time, place and situation for everything. In archery he has gone as far as one can go, he is successful in warding off all manner of attack, most skilled in all arts, and foremost, through his fine achievements, in all crafts. He has a good memory, is intelligent, clever, steady and prudent, versed in all the treatises, has many friends, is wealthy, strong of body, with large limbs, with all his faculties complete, generous to all, dear and pleasant to many. Any work he might undertake he manages to complete, he speaks methodically, shares his great riches with the many, honours what should be honoured, reveres what should be revered, worships what should be worshipped. Would such a person, Subhuti, feel ever-increasing joy and zest ?

Subhuti :   He would, O Lord.

The Lord :   Now suppose, further, that this person, so greatly accomplished, should have taken his family with him on a journey, his mother and father, his sons and daughters. By some circumstance they find themselves in a great, wild forest. The foolish ones among them would feel fright; terror and hairraising fear. He, however, would fearlessly say to his family : "Do not be afraid ! I shall soon take you safely and securely out of this terrible and frightening forest. I shall soon set you free !" If then more and more hostile and inimical forces should rise up against him in that forest, would this heroic man decide to abandon his family, and to take himself alone out of that terrible and frightening forest—he who is not one to draw back, who is endowed with all the force of firmness and vigour, who is wise, exceedingly tender and compassionate, courageous and a master of many resources ?

Subhuti :   No, O Lord. For that person, who does not abandon his family, has at his disposal powerful resources, both within and without. On his side forces will arise in that wild forest which are quite a match for the hostile and inimical forces, and they will stand up for him and protect him. Those enemies and adversaries of his, who look for a weak spot, who seek for a weak spot, will not gain any hold over him. He is competent to deal with the situation, and is able, unhurt and uninjured, soon to take out of that forest, both his family and himself, and securely and safely will they reach a village, city or market town.

The Lord : Just so, Subhuti, is it with a Bodhisattva who is full of pity and concerned with the welfare of all beings, who dwells in friendliness, compassion, sympathetic joy and even-mindedness.

2. DESCRIPTION OF A BODHISATTVA

The hero who can practise the perfection of wisdom is a "Bodhi-sattva", i.e. a "being" who does not live for himself, but only for "enlightenment", his own and that of others. In his essence he is enlightenment, and he strives to become a Buddha, i.e. one who is fully enlightened. The Sutra gives some scholastic definitions of the word "Bodhisattva", which read better in the original Sanskrit than in English. A short descriptive passage is likely to illuminate more clearly the features of the ideal man of the Mahayana.

8.

The Lord : Subhuti, that son or daughter of good family who, as a Bodhisattva, even for one single day remains attentive to the perfection of wisdom, begets a great heap of merit. For, as he goes on dwelling day and night in those mental activities, he becomes more and more worthy of the gifts bestowed on him by all beings. Because no other being has a mind so full of friendliness as he has, except for the Buddhas, the Lords. And the Tathagatas, of course, are matchless, unequalled, endowed with inconceivable dharmas.

How then does that son or daughter of good family at first aspire to that merit ? He becomes endowed with that kind of wise insight which allows him to see all beings as on the way to their slaughter. Great compassion thereby takes hold of him. With his heavenly eye he surveys countless beings, and what he sees fills him with great agitation. So many carry the burden of a karma which will soon be punished in the hells, others have acquired unfortunate rebirths which keep them away from the Buddha and his teachings, others are doomed soon to be killed or they are enveloped in the net of false views, or fail to find the path, while others who had gained a rebirth favourable to their emancipation have lost it again.

And he radiates great friendliness and compassion over all those beings, and gives his attention to them, thinking : "I shall become a saviour to all those beings, I shall release them from all their sufferings !" But he does not make either this, or anything else, into a sign with which he becomes intimate. This also is the great light of a Bodhisattva's wisdom, which allows him to know full enlightenment. For, when they dwell in this dwelling, Bodhisattvas become worthy of the gifts of the whole world, and yet they do not turn back on full enlightenment. When their thoughts are well supported by perfect wisdom and when they are near to all-knowledge, then they purify the gifts of those who give them the requisites of life. Therefore a Bodhisattva should dwell in this mental work associated with perfect wisdom, if he does not want to consume his alms fruitlessly, if he wants to point out the path to all beings, to shed light over a wide range, to set free from birth-and-death all the beings who are subject to it, and to cleanse the organs of vision of all beings.

If he wishes to dwell in mental activities directed towards these goals, he should bring to mind mental activities associated with the perfection of wisdom. For one who decides to bring these to mind, his mind works on the welfare of all beings. But he should give no room to other mental activities, such as lack in perfect wisdom. If he acts so (as the mental work, which is essentially a loving concern for beings, impels him), then he spends his days and nights in mental activities associated with the perfection of wisdom. Suppose a man, well versed in jewelry and the different varieties of jewels, had newly acquired a precious gem. That would make him very glad and elated. If he again lost this precious gem, he would be very sad and distressed. Constantly and always mental activites associated with that jewel would proceed in him, and he would regret to be parted from it. He would not forget it, until he had either regained this gem, or gained another one of like quality and kind. Just so a Bodhisattva who has lost again the precious jewel of perfect wisdom ; with a clear perception of the preciousness of perfect wisdom, and convinced that he has not been definitely parted from it, he should, with a thought that is not lacking in mental work on perfect wisdom, and which is directed to the state of all-knowledge, search about every-where until he has regained this Sutra, or gained an equivalent one. All that time he should be one who is not lacking in mental activities associated with the acquisition of the precious jewel of the perfection of wisdom, one who is not lacking in mental activities associated with the acquisition of the great jewel of all-knowledge.

3. THE RANGE OF COMPASSION

Compassion considers the sufferings of other people, and endeavours to remove them. A Bodhisattva's compassion is particularly intense, and it aims at universality.

9.

Subhuti : Doers of what is hard are the Bodhisattvas who have set out to win full enlightenment. Thanks to the effect which the practice of the six perfections has on them they do not wish to attain release in a private Nirvana of their own. They survey the highly painful world of beings, they want to win full enlightenment, and yet they do not tremble at birth-and-death.

The Lord : So it is Subhuti. Doers of what is hard are the Bodhisattvas who have set out for the benefit and happiness of the world, out of pity for it. "We will become a shelter for the world, a refuge, the place of rest, the final relief, islands, lights and leaders of the world. We will win full enlightenment, and become the resort of the world"—with these words they make a vigorous effort to win full enlightenment.

How then do the Bodhisattvas, awoken to full enlightenment, become the world's shelter ? They protect from all the sufferings which belong to birth-and-death, they struggle and make efforts to rid the world of them.

How do they become the world's refuge ? They set free from birth, decay, illness, death, sorrow, lamentation, pain, sadness and despair those beings who are doomed to undergo these conditions.

How do they become the world's resting place ? The Tathagatas demonstrate Dharma to beings so that they may learn not to embrace anything.

Subhuti : How does that non-embracing come about ?

The Lord : The non-embracing of form, etc., is the same as its non-connection, the same as its non-production and non-stopping. One thus learns not to embrace anything as a result of the cognition and vision that "all dharmas are non-embracing, non-connected".

And how do the Bodhisattvas become the world's final relief ? The state beyond form, etc., is not form, etc. And yet, as the Beyond, so form, etc., and so all dharmas.

Subhuti : If forms, etc., and if all dharmas are the Beyond, then surely the Bodhisattvas must fully know all dharmas. Because there is no discrimination between them.

The Lord : So it is. In that Beyond there is no discrimination. Through their non-discrimination do all dharmas become fully known to the Bodhisattvas. That also is most hard for the Bodhisattvas that they meditate on all dharmas, but neither realise their knowledge (by winning extinction), nor become cowed by them. Their meditation is prompted by the desire to fully know all dharmas, and then, awoken to full enlightenment, to demonstrate and reveal these dharmas.

And how do Bodhisattvas become the world's islands ? "Islands" are pieces of land limited by water, in rivers or lakes. Just so, form etc., is limited at its beginning and end, and so are all dharmas. But the limitation of all dharmas is the same as the Calm Quiet, the Sublime, as Nirvana, the Really Existing, the Unperverted.

And how do they become the world's lights ? Here the Bodhisattvas win full enlightenment, and then they take away all the darkness and gloom of the un-cognition from beings who for so long have been enveloped in the membrane of the shell of ignorance, and overcome by darkness, and they illuminate them through wisdom.

How do they become the world's leaders ? When they have become enlightened, the Bodhisattvas demonstrate Dharma in order to reveal the absence of production and stopping in the essential nature of form, etc., and in the dharmas which constitute and distinguish ordinary people, Disciples, Pratyekabuddhas, Bodhisattvas and Buddhas, and in all dharmas in general.

How are they the world's resort ? When they have become enlightened, the Bodhisattvas demonstrate Dharma by teaching that form, etc., are situated in the world's space. All dharmas are situated in space, they have not come, they have not gone, they are the same as space. Space has not come nor gone, it is not made, nor unmade, nor effected. It has not stood up, does not last, not endure. It is neither produced nor stopped. The same is true of all dharmas which are, after the fashion of space, undiscriminate. Because the emptiness of form, etc., neither comes nor goes. Nor does the emptiness of all dharmas. For all dharmas are situated in emptiness and from that situation they do not depart. They are situated in the Signless, the Wishless, the Ineffective, in non-production, no-birth, in the absence of positivity, in dream and self, in the boundless, in the Calm Quiet, in Nirvana, in the Unrecoverable. They have not come nor gone, situated in immobility. They are situated in form, etc., and in the full enlightenment of Arhats and Pratyekabuddhas.

10.

The Lord : A Bodhisattva is not afraid when he gets into a wilderness infested with wild beasts. For it is his duty to renounce everything for the sake of all beings. Therefore he should react with the thought : "If these wild beasts should devour me, then just that will be my gift to them. The perfection of giving will become more perfect in me, and I will come nearer to full enlightenment. And after I have won full enlightenment I will take steps so that in my Buddhafield there will be no animals at all, that one will have even no conception of them, but that all beings in it will live on heavenly food". Moreover, a Bodhisattva should not be afraid if he finds himself in a wilderness infested with robbers. For Bodhisattvas take pleasure in the wholesome practice of renouncing all their belongings. A Bodhisattva must cast away even his body, and he must renounce all that is necessary to life. He should react to the danger with the thought : "If those beings take away from me everything that is necessary to life, then let that be my gift to them. If someone should rob me of my life, I should feel no ill-will, anger or fury on account of that. Even against them I should take no offensive action, either by body, voice or mind. This will be an occasion to bring the perfections of giving, morality and patience to greater perfection and I will get nearer to full enlightenment. When I have won full enlightenment, I will act and behave in such a way that in my Buddhafield wildernesses infested with robbers will in no way whatsoever either be, or even be conceivable. And my exertions to bring about perfect purity in that Buddhafield will be so great that in it neither these nor other faults will exist, or even be conceivable. Furthermore, in a waterless waste also a Bodhisattva should not be afraid. For his character is such that he is not alarmed or terrified. He should resolve that his own training might result in removing all thirst from all beings. He should not tremble when he thinks that, if he dies from thirst, he will be reborn as a Preta. On the contrary, he should direct a thought of great compassion unto all beings, and think : "Alas, certainly those beings must be of small merit if in their world such deserts are conceivable. After I have won enlightenment, I will see to it that in my Buddhafield no such deserts exist, or are even conceivable. And I will bestow on all beings so much merit that they shall have the most excellent water. Thus will I exert firm vigour on behalf of all beings, so that on that occasion also the perfection of vigour shall become more perfect in me". Furthermore, in a foodless waste also a Bodhisattva should not be afraid. He should arm himself with the thought : "I will exert firm vigour, I will purify my own Buddhafield in such a way that, after I have won enlightenment, in that Buddhafield there will be no foodless wastes, and none will be even conceivable. The beings in that field shall be entirely happy, filled with happiness, possessed of all happiness. And thus will I act that all the intentions and plans of those beings shall be realised. Just as with the Gods of the Thirty-Three an idea in their minds is sufficient to produce anything they may desire, so I will exert firm vigour so that those beings can realise and produce everything by merely thinking it in their minds. In order that their legitimate intentions should be fulfilled, in order that all beings, everywhere and anywhere, should not go short of the requirements of life, I will so struggle for perfect purity in my own thoughts, for the sake of all beings, that on that occasion also the perfection of concentration will become more perfect in me". Furthermore, a Bodhisattva will not be afraid in a district infested by epidemics. But he should consider, reflect and deliberate that "there is no dharma here which sickness could oppress, nor is that which is called 'sickness' a dharma". In that manner he should contemplate emptiness, and he should not be afraid. But he should not think that "it will be an excessively long time before I shall win full enlightenment", and he should not tremble at such a thought. For that thought-moment (which in reality has not been produced), is the extreme limit of something which has no beginning; in other words, it is the absence of a limit. A Bodhisattva should therefore avoid dwelling in his mind on difficulties, and he should think that "great and long is this limit which has no beginning, for it is connected with one single thought-moment; in other words, it is the absence of a limit". This will prevent a Bodhisattva from trembling at the thought that it will be a long time before he will win full enlightenment. Moreover, Subhuti, if these and other fears and terrors, be they due to something seen, heard, felt or known, do not cause a Bodhisattva to tremble, then one should know that this son or daughter of good family is capable of knowing full enlightenment. A Bodhisattva should therefore put on the great armour of the thought : "Thus will I act, thus will I exert firm vigour that, after I have won full enlightenment, all beings in my Buddhafield shall not suffer from sickness, and shall not even know what it is. I will act in such a way that I shall preach what the Tathagatas have taught, and that I will do what I have preached. And I will so master the perfection of wisdom, for the sake of all beings, that on that occasion also the perfection of wisdom will in me come to fulfilment !"

11.

Subhuti : What is the manifestation of the great compassion?

The Lord : That the Bodhisattva, the great being, who courses on the Bodhisattva-pilgrimage, thinks that "for the sake of the weal of every single being will I, dwelling in the hells for aeons countless like the sands of the Ganges, experience therein the cuttings up, the breakings up, the poundings, the torments, the roastings, until that being has become established in the Buddha-cognition". This excessive fortitude, this indefatigability, for the sake of all beings, that is called the manifestation of the great compassion.

12.

The Lord : A Bodhisattva, a great being, after he has produced an adamantine thought, will cause a great mass of beings, a great collection of beings, to achieve the highest.

Subhuti : What is the production of an adamantine thought ?

The Lord : Here the Bodhisattva produces a thought thus : "After I have put on the armour in the immeasurable stream of birth-and-death, I should become one who never abandons all-beings. Towards all beings should I adopt the same attitude of mind. All beings I should lead to Nirvana by means of the three vehicles. But even when I have led all beings into Nirvana, no being at all has been led to Nirvana. For one should look through to the fact that all dharmas are neither produced nor stopped. With my thought exclusively on the knowledge of all modes should I course in the six perfections. Everywhere should I train myself to accomplish a penetration into all dharmas. I should penetrate to the consummation of the one principle of all dharmas. For the sake of the penetration to the consummation of the perfections should I train myself in all dharmas, for the sake of penetrating to the consummation of the Unlimited, of the trances, the formless attainments, the super-knowledges, of the ten powers, the grounds of self-confidence, the special Buddha-dharmas". This is the production of an adamantine thought by the Bodhisattva, the great being. Supported thereon the Bodhisattva will cause a great mass of beings, a great collection of beings, to achieve the highest ; and that without depending on anything. Moreover, a Bodhisattva produces a thought thus : "For the sake of as many beings as have painful feelings in the hells, among the animals, or in the world of Yama, for their sake I will have the same painful feelings". With regard to this a Bodhisattva should produce a thought thus : "For the sake of each single being will I experience for hundreds of thousands of Niyutas of Kotis of aeons the pains of the hells, of the animal world, of the world of Yama, until those beings will have become released in the realm of Nirvana which leaves nothing behind. That will be my skill in means. Afterwards I will, for the sake of my own self, having planted wholesome roots for hundreds of thousands of Niyutas of Kotis of aeons, and having become equipped for enlightenment, fully awake to the utmost right and perfect enlightenment". This is the production of an adamantine thought by the Bodhisattva, the great being.

4.   SKILL IN MEANS
Skill in means is often lauded in these texts.   As a bird needs

two wings to maintain itself in the air, so a Bodhisattva needs
both wisdom and skill in means to hold himself up in emptiness.
The Bodhisattva has a keen understanding of the inclinations,
aptitudes and problems of different individuals; he is resourceful
in adapting himself to their needs, and in devising for their
salvation methods which suit their particular bend. Since the
whole point of "skill in means" lies in its application to concrete
situations, a general description is bound to remain inadequate.
The second extract (No. 14) describes the life of a Bodhisattva
on the eighth stage. One distinguishes ten stages of a Bodhisattva's
progress, from the time that he has decided to win enlightenment
for himself and for others, up to Buddhahood. On the seventh
stage a full understanding of wisdom is attained (see B Iv, 1, No.
55), and that, on the eighth stage, bears fruit in "skill in means".

13.

Sakra : A great lore is this perfection of wisdom, a lore
without measure, a quite measureless lore, an unsurpassed lore,
an unequalled lore, a lore which equals the unequalled.

The Lord: So it is, Kausika. For thanks to this lore, i.e.
the perfection of wisdom, the Buddhas of the past have won full
enlightenment. Thanks to it the Buddhas of the future will
know it. Thanks to it, the Buddhas of the present do know it.
Thanks to it I have known it. Thanks to just this lore do the
ten wholesome ways of acting become manifest in the world,
the four trances and the four Unlimited, associated with the
limbs of enlightenment, the four formless attainments upheld
by the limbs of enlightenment, the six super-knowledges
associated with the limbs of enlightenment, the thirty-seven
dharmas which constitute the limbs of enlightenment, in short
the 84,000 articles of dharma, the cognition of the Buddha,
the cognition of the Self-Existent, the inconceivable cognition.
But when there are no Tathagatas in the world, then it is the
Bodhisattvas,—endowed with skill in means as a result of their
having heard the outpouring of the perfection of wisdom in
the past (when there were Buddhas), full of pity for beings,
come into this world out of pity,—who foster in the world the
ten wholesome ways of acting, the four Trances, the four
Unlimited, the four formless attainments, the five super-
knowledges, but all dissociated from the limbs of enlightenment.
Just as thanks to the disk of the moon all the herbs, stars and

constellations are illumined according to their power and strength, so, after the Tathagata has passed away and his good Dharma has disappeared, in the absence of the Tathagatas, whatever righteous, upright, outstanding, or wholesome life is conceived and manifested in the world, all that has come forth from the Bodhisattva, has been brought forth by him, has spread from his skill in means. But the skill in means of the Bodhisattvas should be known as having come forth from the perfection of wisdom.

14.

The Lord : On the eighth stage a Bodhisattva enters into the thoughts of all beings : with one single thought he recognizes the thoughts and mental activities of all beings. He further plays with the super-knowledges : i.e. playing with these super-knowledges, he passes on from Buddhafield to Buddhafield. But, though he has a vision of the Buddha, he does not form the notion of a Buddha. He further has a vision of Buddhafields, i.e. abiding in just one Buddhafield, he sees innumerable Buddhafields, and yet he does not form the notion of a Buddhafield. He further creates Buddhafields in accordance with what he has seen. That means that he renounces the great trichiliocosm, after he has occupied the position of its Ruler, or that of a universal monarch, but without feeling any conceit about that. He further honours the Buddhas, i.e. he honours the Dharma, as being a help to all beings. He contemplates the Buddha-body as it really is, which means that he contemplates the Dharma-body as it really is.

Furthermore, he has a cognition of the higher and lower faculties of others, in other words, it is one of the ten powers that he has a wise cognition of the extent to which the faculties of all beings are perfected. He further purifies the Buddhafield, i.e. he purifies the thoughts of all beings, without taking them as a basis. He further concentrates on everything as an illusion, i.e. absorbed in this concentration a Bodhisattva performs all works, although his thought does not proceed in any dharma. He is perpetually immersed in this concentration, because it comes to him as a reward of the good deeds of his past. His personality further becomes more perfect as the spiritual quality of the beings around him improves. He takes hold of a personality at will, to the extent that a maturing of beings takes place. And it is through the maturing of all beings that he gains a personality at will.

5. No Possessiveness About Merit

A Bodhisattva's practices are a source of great merit to him (see A V). The acquisition of merit is an essential prerequisite to the extinction of selfhood, but it also is a source of danger to it. One may treat merit as a field of personal accumulation, like a bank-account, and one may begrudge others their spiritual attainments, so as to compare oneself favourably with them. The taint of possessiveness is removed from merit by two procedures which are respectively known as "Rejoicing" and as "Turning over of merit". First of all, just as one should react to the sufferings of others with compassion, so their happiness should evoke "sympathetic joy". This ancient Buddhist virtue, by which one enters into a joyous sympathy with the prosperity of others, appears in our Sutras as a "Rejoicing" or "Jubilation" over the merits and spiritual perfections of others. Secondly, merit is that quality in us which ensures future benefits to us, be they material or spiritual. A Bodhisattva should be willing to give up his own store of merit for the happiness of others, and dedicate it to the cause of the enlightenment of all beings.

15.

Subhuti : How should a Bodhisattva who is only just beginning, stand in perfect wisdom, how train himself ?

The Lord : Such a Bodhisattva should tend, love and honour the good friends. His good friends are those who will instruct and admonish him in perfect wisdom, and who will expound to him its meaning. They will expound it as follows : "Come here, son of good family, make endeavours in the six perfections. And whatever you may have achieved by way of giving gifts, of guarding your morality, of perfecting yourself in patience, of exertion in vigour, of entering into concentration, or of mastery in wisdom,—all that you must dedicate to full enlightenment. But do not misconstrue full enlightenment as form, or any other skandhas. For all-knowledge is intangible".

16.

Sakra : The sons or daughters of good family who rejoice at

the productions of thought of those Bodhisattvas who have just begun to set out in the vehicle, as well as of those who progress on the course, who rejoice at the nature of those who are irreversible, as well as of those who are bound to one more birth only,—to what extent is their merit a superior one ?

The Lord : It would be easier to measure Sumeru, king of mountains, or a world system, up to a great trichiliocosm, with the help of a tip of straw, then to measure the extent of that merit.

Sakra : Beset by Mara are those beings who do not come to hear of this immeasurable merit of that jubilation over the career of a Bodhisattva,—which begins with the first thought of enlightenment, and which ends with full enlightenment,— who do not know it, who do not see it, who do not bring that jubilation to mind. They are partisans of Mara, deceased in the realms of Mara. For those who have brought to mind those thoughts, who have turned them over into the supreme enlightenment, have rejoiced at them, they have done so in order to shatter Mara's world. One should, O Lord, rejoice at the various stages of the thought which the Bodhisattvas have raised to enlightenment. Sons and daughters of good family, who have not abandoned the Tathagata, the Dharma, and the Community, they should rejoice in those stages of the thought of enlightenment.

The Lord : So it is, Kausika. And those sons and daughters of good family, who have rejoiced in the stages of the thought of enlightenment, they shall,—whether they belong to the vehicle of the Bodhisattvas, or that of the Pratyekabuddhas, or that of the Disciples—soon please the Tathagatas, and not displease them.

Sakra : So it is, O Lord. Therefore, wherever they may be reborn as a result of the wholesome roots (they have planted), when their hearts were filled with jubilation, there they shall be treated with respect, revered, worshipped and adored. They shall never see any unpleasant sights, nor hear any unpleasant sounds, nor smell any unpleasant smells, nor taste any unpleasant tastes, nor come into contact with anything unpleasant to touch. One must expect them to be reborn in the heavens, and not in the states of woe. For they have rejoiced in the wholesome roots of countless beings, roots which bring happiness to all beings. The thoughts of jubilation of those who, after they have produced an urge towards enlightenment, have rejoiced over the successive stages of the thought of enlightenment in persons who belong to the vehicle of the Bodhisattvas, shall, as they grow, become the nourishers of full enlightenment. After they who rejoiced have won full enlightenment, they also shall lead countless beings to Nirvana.

The Lord : So it is, Kausika, as you have said it, through the Tathagata's might. The wholesome roots of countless beings are rejoiced over, planted and consummated as a consequence of the action of a son or daughter of good family who has rejoiced over the successive stages of the thought of enlightenment in those persons who belong to the vehicle of the Bodhisattvas.

17.

Subhuti : A Bodhisattva, a great being, considers the world with its ten directions, in every direction, extending everywhere. He considers the world systems, quite immeasurable, quite beyond reckoning, quite measureless, quite inconceivable, infinite and boundless.

He considers in the past period, in each single direction, in each single world system, the Tathagatas, quite immeasurable, quite beyond reckoning, quite measureless, quite inconceivable, infinite and boundless, who have won final Nirvana in the realm of Nirvana which leaves nothing behind,—their tracks cut off, their course cut off, their obstacles annulled, guides through (the world of) becoming, their tears dried up, with all their impediments crushed, their own burdens laid down, with their own weal reached, in whom the fetters of becoming are extinguished, whose thoughts are well freed by right understanding, and who have attained to the highest perfection in the control of their entire hearts.

He considers them, from where they began with the production of the thought of enlightenment, proceeding to the time when they won full enlightenment, until they finally entered Nirvana in the realm of Nirvana which leaves nothing behind, and the whole span of time up to the vanishing of the good Dharma (as preached by each one of these Tathagatas).

He considers the mass of morality, the mass of concentration, the mass of wisdom, the mass of emancipation, the mass of the vision and cognition of emancipation of those Buddhas and Lords.

In addition he considers the store of merit associated with the six perfections, with the achievement of the qualities of a Buddha, and with the perfections of self-confidence and of the powers ; and also those associated with the perfection of the superknowledges, of comprehension, of the vows ; and the store of merit associated with the accomplishment of the cognition of the all-knowing, with the solicitude for beings, the great friendliness and the great compassion, and the immeasurable and incalculable Buddha-qualities.

And also the full enlightenment and its happiness, and the perfection of the sovereignty over all dharmas, and the accomplishment of the measureless and unconquered supreme wonderworking power which has conquered all, and the power of the Tathagata's cognition of what is truly real, which is without covering, attachment or obstruction, unequalled, equal to the unequalled, incomparable, without measure, and the power of the Buddha-cognition pre-eminent among the powers, and the vision and cognition of a Buddha, the perfection of the ten powers, the obtainment of that supreme ease which results from the four grounds of self-confidence and the obtainment of Dharma through the realization of the ultimate reality of all dharmas.

He also considers the turning of the wheel of Dharma, the carrying of the torch of Dharma, the beating of the drum of Dharma, the filling up of the conch-shell of Dharma, the sounding of the conch-shell of Dharma, the wielding of the sword of Dharma, the pouring down of the rain of Dharma, the offering of the sacrifice of Dharma, the refreshment of all beings through the gift of Dharma, through its presentation to them. He further considers the store of merit of all those who are educated and trained by those demonstrations of Dharma,—whether they concern the dharmas of Buddhas, or those of Pratyekabuddhas, or of Disciples,—who believe in them, who are fixed on them, who are bound to end up in full enlightenment.

He also considers the store of merit, associated with the six perfections, of all those Bodhisattvas of whom those Buddhas and Lords have predicted full enlightenment. He considers the store of merit of all those persons who belong to the Pratyekabuddha-vehicle, and of whom the enlightenment of a Pratyekabuddha has been predicted. He considers the meritorious work founded on giving, morality and meditational development of those who belong to the Disciple-vehicle, and the roots of good with blemish,[1] of those who are still in training, as well as the unblemished[2] roots of good of the adepts.

He considers the roots of good which the common people have planted as a result of the teaching of those Tathagatas. He considers the meritorious work, founded on giving, morality and meditational development, of the four assemblies of those Buddhas and Lords, i.e. of the monks and nuns, the laymen and laywomen. He considers the roots of good planted during all that time by Gods, Nagas, Yakshas, Gandharvas, Asuras, Garudas, Kinnaras and Mahoragas, by men and ghosts, and also by animals, at the time when those Buddhas and Lords demonstrated the Dharma, and when they entered Parinirvana, and when they had entered Parinirvana—thanks to the Buddha, the Lord, thanks to the Dharma, thanks to the Samgha, and thanks to persons of right mind-culture.

(In his meditation the Bodhisattva) piles up the roots of good of all those, all that quantity of merit without exception or remainder, rolls it into one lump, weighs it, and rejoices over it with the most excellent and sublime jubilation, the highest and utmost jubilation, with none above it, unequalled, equalling the unequalled. Having thus rejoiced, he would utter the remark : "I turn over into full enlightenment the meritorious work founded on jubilation. May it feed the full enlightenment, (of myself and of all beings !)"

III. MORAL AND KARMIC QUALIFICATIONS

The persons capable of acting on the precepts of the perfection of wisdom must have certain qualifications, moral or spiritual (No. 18,) and karmic (No. 19). Greed and hate must in such a person be already greatly attenuated, before even a beginning can be made. A detailed explanation of the regular practices by which Buddhists try to weaken anger and greed lies outside the scope of these Sutras. There are, however, a few remarks about considerations liable to counteract anger (No. 20, 21), and about the attitude which a Bodhisattva, who is not a monk, should adopt to sense-desires in those cases where life as a house-holder increases his temptations (No. 22-24).

---

[1] Literally : with outflows.   [2] Literally ; without outflows.

18.

Subhuti : How should a Bodhisattva behave, how should he train if he wants to go forth to supreme enlightenment ?

The Lord : The Bodhisattva should adopt the same attitude towards all beings, his mind should be even towards all beings, he should not handle others with an uneven mind, but with a mind which is friendly, well-disposed, helpful, free from aversion avoiding harm and hurt, he should handle others as if they were his mother, father, son or daughter. As a saviour of all beings should a Bodhisattva behave towards all beings. So should he train himself if he wants to know full enlightenment. He should, himself, stand in the abstention from all evil, he should give gifts, guard his morality, perfect himself in patience, exert vigour, enter into the trances, achieve mastery over wisdom, and he should survey conditioned co-production, both in direct and in reverse order ; and also others he should instigate to do the same, incite and encourage them. He must meditate on the truths, attain to the stage when he reaches the certainty that it is as a Bodhisattva that he will be saved, to the stage where he matures beings, and also others he should instigate to do the same, incite and encourage them. When he longs eagerly for all that and trains himself in it, then everything will be uncovered to him, from form to the established order of Dharma.

19.

Sariputra : Bodhisattvas who are reborn here, and will here resolutely believe in this deep perfection of wisdom, without hesitation, doubt or stupefaction,—where have they deceased and for how long have they practised, they who will follow the doctrine of this perfection of wisdom, understand its meaning, and instruct others in it ?

The Lord : One should know that such a Bodhisattva is reborn here after he has deceased in other world systems where he has honoured and questioned the Buddhas, the Lords. Any Bodhisattva who, after he has deceased in other world systems where he had honoured and questioned the Buddhas, the Lords, is reborn here, would, when he hears this deep perfection of wisdom being taught, identify it with the Teacher, and be convinced that he is face to face with the Teacher, that he has seen the Teacher. When the perfection of wisdom is being taught, he listens attentively, pays respect to it before he hears it, and does not cut the story short.   Such a Bodhisattva should be known as one who has practised for long, who has honoured many Buddhas.

20.

The Lord : The quarrels, contentions and contradictions of those who oppose my Dharma will simply vanish away ;   the intentions of the opponents will remain unfulfilled.   Because it is a fact that for the follower of perfect wisdom those disputes will simply vanish away, and will not abide.   There is a herb, Maghi by name, a cure for all poison.   Suppose a viper, famished, were to see a creature and pursue it, following the scent, in order to eat it ;   but if that creature went to a patch of that herb and stood there, then the smell of that herb would cause the snake to turn back.   Because the healing quality of that herb is so powerful that it overpowers the viper's poison. Just so will the quarrels, contentions and contradictions to which the follower of perfect wisdom is exposed be stilled and appeased, through the piercing flame of perfect wisdom, through its power, its might, through impregnation with its power.   They will vanish, and not grow, nor abide.   And why ? Because it is perfect wisdom which appeases all evil and does not increase it, beginning with ordinary greed up to the attempt to seize on Nirvana as one's own personal property.   And the Gods, and all the Buddhas, and all the Bodhisattvas, will protect this follower of perfect wisdom.   This will be an advantage even here and now.   Moreover, the speech of the follower of perfect wisdom will be acceptable, soft, measured and adequate.   Wrath and conceit will not overpower him. Because perfect wisdom tames and transforms him.   Wrath and conceit he does not increase.   Neither enmity nor ill-will take hold of him, not even a tendency towards them.   He will be mindful and friendly.   He reflects : "If I foster ill-will in myself, my faculties will go to pieces, my features will be consumed, and it is in any case quite illogical that I, who have set out for full enlightenment, and who want to train myself for it, should come under the sway of wrath".   In this way he will quickly regain his mindfulness.   This will be another advantage even here and now.

21.

The Lord : As to the person who belongs to the vehicle of

the Bodhisattvas and who has quarrelled with someone else who also belongs to the vehicle of the Bodhisattvas,—if he does not confess his fault, does not promise restraint in future, harbours a latent bias towards hate, and dwells tied to that bias,—of that person I do not teach the escape from the consequences of his action, and its after-effects will bother him for a long time. But I teach his escape if he confesses his fault, promises restraint in future, and reflects as follows : "I, whose duty it is to drive away, to pacify and appease the quarrels, disputes and conflicts of all beings, I myself engage in disputes ! It is indeed a loss to me, and not a gain, that I should answer back as I am spoken to. When I should be to all beings a bridge across the sea of birth-and-death, I nevertheless say to another, 'The same to you', or return a harsh and rough answer. This is not the way in which I should speak. In fights, quarrels and disputes I should behave like a senseless idiot, or like a dumb sheep. When I hear someone using offensive, abusive, insulting words towards me, my heart should not cherish malice for others. It is not meet and proper for me to perceive the faults of others, or to think that what is being said about the faults of others is worth listening to. For I, since I am earnestly intent on full enlightenment, should not do harm to others. When I should make all beings happy by giving them everything that brings happiness, when I should lead them to Nirvana after having won full enlightenment,—yet nevertheless I bear ill-will ! I should not bear ill-will even against those who have offended against me, and I must avoid getting into a rage, and I must make a firm effort in this direction. Even when my life is in danger I must not get into a rage, and no frown should appear on my face". This is the attitude which a Bodhisattva should adopt also towards persons who belong to the vehicle of the Disciples. Never to get angry with any being, that is the attitude of mind one should adopt towards all beings.

22.

The Lord : Furthermore, an irreversible Bodhisattva does not attach weight to a name, nor to renown, title or fame. He does not get attached to a (particular) name, (which in any case is absent in emptiness). His mind remains undismayed, and interested only in the welfare of all beings. Whether he goes out or comes back, his mind does not wander, and he remains ever mindful. When he lives the life of a householder, he has no great love for pleasant things, and he does not want them too much. With fear and disgust he possesses all pleasant things. Situated in a wilderness infested with robbers one would eat one's meals in fear, and not with repose, with the constant thought of getting away, of getting out of this wilderness. Just so an irreversible Bodhisattva, who lives the life of a householder, simply possesses any pleasant things he may have without caring for them, without eagerness, without attachment. He is not one of those persons who care for dear and pleasant forms. Those who live the life of householders, and who are involved in the five kinds of sensuous pleasures, do not earn their living in an irregular way, but in the right way. Neither do they incur death in a state of sin, nor do they inflict injuries on others. For they have incited all beings to win the supreme happiness,—those worthy men, those great men, supermen, excellent men, splendid men, bulls of men, sublime men, valiant men, heroes of men, leaders of men, water lilies of men, lotuses of men, thoroughbred men, Nagas of men, lions of men, trainers of men ! It is in this spirit that Bodhisattvas live the life of householders, inasmuch as they have been impregnated with the power of the perfection of wisdom.

23.

The Lord : The Gods, right up to the Akanishtha Gods, are enraptured because the Bodhisattva shuns sexual intercourse. From the first thought of enlightenment onwards the Bodhisattva is chaste. He reflects that "one who is not chaste, who pursues sensuous pleasures, causes an obstacle to rebirth even in the Brahma-world; how much more to supreme enlightenment". Therefore, then, a Bodhisattva, chaste, not unchaste, should, having left his home, know full enlightenment.

Sariputra; Does, then, the Bodhisattva in all circumstances have mother and father, wives, sons, paternal and maternal relatives ?

The Lord : Some of the Bodhisattvas do have mother and father, wives, sons, and relatives. Some of them, from the first thought of enlightenment onwards, take chastity upon themselves, and, coursing in the course of a Bodhisattva just as Crown Princes, know full enlightenment. Some Bodhisattvas taste the five sense qualities from skill in means, then leave home and know full enlightenment.   Just as a clever magician or magician's apprentice, well trained in magical illusions, would conjure up the five sense-qualities, delight in them, play with them, minister to them.   What do you think, Sariputra, would that magician, or magician's apprentice, have actually tasted and relished those five sense-qualities ?

Sariputra : No, Lord.

The Lord : Just so do Bodhisattvas, through their skill in means, taste the five kinds of sense-qualities, for the sake of maturing beings.   But they are not stained by the sense-qualities.   Sense desires are disparaged by the Bodhisattva with the words : "Set on fire are sense desires, disgusting are sense desires, murderous are sense desires, enemies are the sense desires !"   It is in such a spirit that a Bodhisattva, for the sake of maturing beings, lays hold of the five sense qualities.

24.

A Voice : You should not follow your teacher from motives of worldly gain, but from desire for Dharma, out of respect for Dharma.   You must also see through Mara's deeds.   For there is always Mara, the Evil One, who may suggest that your teacher tends, enjoys and honours things that can be seen, heard, smelled, tasted, or touched, when in actual fact he does so from skill in means, and has already risen above them.   You should therefore not lose confidence in him, but say to yourself : "I do not know that skill in means as he wisely knows it.   He tends, enjoys and honours those dharmas in order to discipline beings, in order to win wholesome roots for them.   For no attachment to objective supports exists in Bodhisattvas".

IV.   Obstacles

Inability to practise perfect wisdom, or opposition to its teachings are due to lack of effort, bad karma inherited from the past, and the hostility of Mara.

25.

Subhuti : It is hard to gain confidence in the perfection of wisdom if one is unpractised, lacks in wholesome roots and is in the hands of a bad teacher.

The Lord : So it is, Subhuti. It is hard to gain confidence in the perfection of wisdom if one is unpractised, has only diminutive wholesome roots, is dull-witted, does not care, has learned little, has an inferior kind of wisdom, relies on bad teachers, is not eager to learn, unwilling to ask questions and unpractised in wholesome exercises.

Subhuti: How deep, then, is this perfection of wisdom, since it is so hard to gain confidence in it ?

The Lord : Form is neither bound nor freed, because it has no own-being. The past starting point of a material process (=form) is neither bound nor freed, because it is without own-being. The end of a material process, in the future, is neither bound nor freed, because it is without own-being. A present material process is without own-being, because the fact of being present is not a part of the own-being of the present form. And so for the remaining skandhas.

Subhuti : It is hard, it is exceedingly hard, to gain confidence in the perfection of wisdom, if one is unpractised, has planted no wholesome roots, is in the hands of a bad teacher, has come under the sway of Mara, is lazy, of little vigour, poor in memory and stupid.

26.

The Lord : It is quite possible that some Bodhisattvas, although they have seen many hundreds, many thousands, many hundreds of thousands of Buddhas, and have led the holy life in their presence, might nevertheless have no faith in the perfection of wisdom: The reason is that in the past they also have had no respect for this deep perfection of wisdom when, in the presence of those Buddhas and Lords, it was taught. Because they lacked in respect for it, they had no desire to learn more about it, did not honour it, were unwilling to ask questions, and lacked in faith. Lacking in faith they thereupon walked out of the assemblies. It is because in the past they have produced, accumulated, piled up and collected karma conducive to the ruin of Dharma that also at present they walk out when this deep perfection of wisdom is being taught. From lack of respect without faith and firm belief in the perfection of wisdom, they have no concord either in their bodies or in their thoughts. Devoid of concord they do not know, see, recognise or make known this perfection of wisdom. First, they do not believe, then they do not hear, then they do not see, then they do not recognise it, and thus they produce, accumulate, pile up and collect karma conducive to the ruin of the Dharma. This in its turn will bring about karma conducive to weakness in wisdom. That in its turn will make them refuse, reject and revile this perfection of wisdom when it is being taught, and, having rejected it, they will walk out. But by rejecting this perfection of wisdom they reject the all-knowledge of the Buddhas and Lords, past, future and present. Not content with having vitiated their own continuities, they will, as if all aflame, deter, dissuade, turn away others also,— persons of small intelligence, wisdom, merit and wholesome roots, endowed with but a little faith, affection, serenity, and desire-to-do, beginners, essentially unqualified,—trying to take away even that little faith, affection, serenity and desire-to-do. They will say that one should not train in it, they will declare that it is not the Buddha's word. They first vitiate and estrange their own continuities, and then those of others. Thereby they will calumniate the perfection of wisdom. To calumniate the perfection of wisdom means to calumniate all-knowledge, and therewith the past, future and present Buddhas. They will be removed from the presence of the Buddhas and Lords, deprived of the Dharma, expelled from the Samgha. In each and every way they will be shut out from the Triple Jewel . . .

Subhuti : For what reason do these people believe that they should oppose this perfection of wisdom ?

The Lord : Such a person is beset by Mara. His karma is conducive to weakness in wisdom, and so he has no faith or serene confidence in deep dharmas. Endowed with these two evil dharmas he will oppose this perfection of wisdom. More-over, Subhuti, that person will be one who is in the hands of bad teachers ; or he may be one who has not practised ; or one who has settled down in the skandhas ; or one who exalts himself and deprecates others, looking out for faults. Endowed with also these four attributes will be that person who believes that this perfection of wisdom should be opposed when it is being taught.

27.

Subhuti : Deep, O Lord, is perfect wisdom. It is a heap of treasure. It is a pure heap, sharing in the purity of space.

It would not be surprising if many obstacles should arise to someone who takes up, learns and studies this perfection of wisdom.

The Lord : There will be many obstacles to the study of this perfection of wisdom. For Mara, the Evil One, will make great efforts to cause difficulties. Therefore one should hurry up with one's task of copying it out. If one has one month to do it in, or two months, or three months, one should just carry on with the writing. If one has a year or more, even then one should just carry on with writing this perfection of wisdom, (since after, or even during, that time one may be prevented by all kinds of interruptions). Because it is a fact that in respect of very precious things many difficulties are wont to arise.

Subhuti : Here, O Lord, when the perfection of wisdom is being studied, Mara the Evil One will in many ways show zeal, and exert himself to cause difficulties.

The Lord : In spite of that he is powerless to cause really effective obstacles to a Bodhisattva who gives his undivided attention to his task.

Sariputra : If, O Lord, Mara the Evil One is determined to cause obstacles to the study of this perfection of wisdom, how can people actually study it just now, and through whose might can they do so ?

The Lord : It is through the might of the Buddhas and Lords, of the Tathagatas, that they study it, and that they make progress in training in Thusness. For it is in the nature of things that the Buddhas, the Lords, who stand, hold and maintain themselves in countless world systems, should bring to mind and uphold everyone who teaches and studies this perfection of wisdom. The Buddhas will bring him to mind and assist him. And it is quite impossible to cause an obstacle to someone who has been brought to mind and upheld by the Buddhas.

Sariputra : It is through the Buddha's might, sustaining power and grace that Bodhisattvas study this deep perfection of wisdom, and progressively train in Thusness ?

The Lord : So it is, Sariputra. They are known to the Tathagata, they are sustained and seen by the Tathagata, and the Tathagata beholds them with his Buddha-eye. And those Bodhisattvas who study this perfection of wisdom, and who are progressively training in Thusness, they are near to the Thusness of the supreme enlightenment, and they stand poised in their decision to win full enlightenment. If they only just study this perfection of wisdom, without progressively training in Thusness, they will not stand poised in Suchness in the supreme enlightenment. But nevertheless they also are known to the Tathagata, sustained and seen by the Tathagata, and the Tathagata beholds them with his Buddha-eye. That continual study of the perfection of wisdom, and the mental excitation about it, will be greatly profitable to them, a great advantage, fruit and reward. For, as aiming at ultimate reality, the perfection of wisdom has been set up for the penetration by all beings into what all dharmas truly are.

28.

Subhuti : What then, O Lord, is the reason why Mara makes these great efforts and bestirs himself to prevent, by this or that device, people from learning and studying this perfection of wisdom ?

The Lord : Perfect wisdom is the source of the all-knowledge of the Buddhas, the Lords. And that in its turn is the source of the religion of the Tathagatas, which leads countless beings to forsake their defilements. But to those who have forsaken the defilements Mara cannot gain entry, and that makes him distressed and dispirited, and the dart of sorrow vexes him. In consequence, when this perfection of wisdom is being written and studied, he makes in his great tribulation a great effort, and bestirs himself, with this or that device, to prevent the study of this perfection of wisdom.

29.

Sakra : It is wonderful, O Lord, it is astonishing, O Well-Gone ! As contrary to the whole world is this Dharma demonstrated. It has been preached so that dharmas should not be taken up, but the world is determined to take up dharmas.

30.

The Lord : With their Buddha-eye the Tathagatas who at present reside in countless world systems behold the Bodhisattva who courses in perfect wisdom, and they help him, and bring him to mind. It is quite certain, Subhuti, that Bodhisattvas who course in perfect wisdom, and who are helped and brought

to mind by the Tathagatas, are irreversible from full enlightenment. No obstacle, put up by Mara, or anyone else, can stop
them. Even if all beings in the great trichiliocosm should
become evil Maras, and if each one of them would conjure up
just as many diabolic armies, then even they all together would
not have the strength to obstruct on his way to full enlightenment that Bodhisattva who is brought to mind by the Buddhas,
and who courses in perfect wisdom. And that would remain
true even if all the beings in all the countless trichiliocosms
should become evil Maras, and if each one of them should
conjure up just as many diabolic armies. The endowment
with two dharmas safeguards a Bodhisattva against all attacks
from the Maras, or their hosts : He does not abandon any
being, and he surveys all dharmas from emptiness. Two other
dharmas have the same effect : As he speaks so he acts, and he
is brought to mind by the Buddhas, the Lords.

V. MERIT FROM PERFECT WISDOM

*A great deal of space is given over in the Prajñāpāramitā
Sutras to the merit gained from devotion to perfect wisdom.
Three extracts will be sufficient to indicate the gist of these
passages.*

31.

The Lord : When he trains in the perfection of wisdom, a
Bodhisattva trains in that which is the highest possible degree
of perfection for any being. For his merit is the greatest
possible. Subhuti, if you consider all the beings in the great
trichiliocosm, are there many ?

Subhuti : Even in Jambudvipa alone there are many beings,
how many more would there be in the great trichiliocosm !

The Lord : If one single Bodhisattva were, during his entire
life, to furnish all those beings with robes, alms bowl, lodging,
medicinal appliances for use in sickness, and all that brings
them happiness,— would such a Bodhisattva on the strength of
that beget a great deal of merit ?

Subhuti : He would, O Lord.

The Lord : A much greater merit still would that Bodhisattva
beget who would develop this perfection of wisdom for even the
duration of a finger-snap. So greatly profitable is the perfection
of wisdom of the Bodhisattvas, because she feeds the supreme

enlightenment. A Bodhisattva should therefore train in perfect wisdom if he wants to know full enlightenment, to arrive at the supreme position among all beings, to become a protector of the helpless, to reach the sphere of a Buddha, to emulate the manliness of a Buddha, to sport with a Buddha's sport, to roar a Buddha's lion roar, to reach the accomplishment of a Buddha, and to explain the Dharma in the great trichiliocosm. When a Bodhisattva trains in the perfection of wisdom, I do not see the accomplishment in which he has not been trained.

32.

The Lord : If I were, Subhuti, to teach the heap of merit of those sons and daughters of good family, and how great a heap of merit those sons and daughters of good family will at that time beget and acquire, beings who listen to this would become frantic and perplexed. Just as this discourse on Dharma has by the Tathagata been taught as inconceivable and incomparable, so one should expect just an inconceivable reward from it.

33.

The Lord : That spot of earth, Subhuti, where one has taken from this discourse on Dharma but one stanza of four verses, taught it or illuminated it, that spot of earth will be like a shrine for the whole world with its Gods, men and Asuras. What then should we say of those who will bear in mind this discourse on Dharma in its entirety, who will recite it, study it, and illuminate it in full detail for others ? Most wonderfully blest, O Subhuti, they will be. And in that spot of earth, Subhuti, either the Teacher dwells, or a sage representing him.

B. THE DHARMA

In the Gnosis of perfect wisdom, subject and object are identical. Nevertheless, for the purposes of description, one can distinguish between perfect wisdom as a subjective, mental function (I—III), and its object, which is emptiness (IV).

I. PRAISE OF PERFECT WISDOM

The Prajñāpāramitā Sutras contain a number of litanies in praise of perfect wisdom, of which I quote here the least technical one.

34.

Sariputra : The perfection of wisdom, O Lord, is the accomplishment of the cognition of the all-knowing. The perfection of wisdom is the state of all-knowledge.

The Lord : So it is, Sariputra, as you say.

Sariputra : The perfection of wisdom gives light, O Lord, I pay homage to the perfection of wisdom ! She is worthy of homage. She is unstained, and the entire world cannot stain her. She is a source of light, and from everyone in the triple world she removes darkness, and leads them away from the blinding darkness caused by defilements and wrong views. In her we can find shelter. Most excellent are all her works. She makes us seek the safety of the wings of enlightenment. She brings light to the blind, so that all fear and distress may be forsaken. She has gained the five eyes, and she shows the path to all beings. She herself is an organ of vision. She disperses the gloom and darkness of delusion. She does nothing about all dharmas. She guides to the Path those who have strayed on to a bad road. She is identical with all-knowledge. She never produces any dharma, because she has forsaken the residues relating to both kinds of coverings, those produced by defilement and those produced by the cognizable. She does not stop any dharma. Herself unstopped and unproduced is the perfection of wisdom. She is the Mother of the Bodhisattvas on account of the emptiness of own-marks. As the donor of the jewel of all the Buddha-dharmas she brings about the ten powers of a Tathagata. She cannot be crushed. She protects the unprotected, with the help of the four grounds of self-confidence. She is the antidote to birth-and-death. She has a clear knowledge of the own-being of all dharmas, for she does not stray away from it. The perfection of wisdom of the Buddhas, the Lords, sets in motion the wheel of Dharma.

II. THE SIX PERFECTIONS

The perfection of wisdom cannot be understood apart from the other five perfections. The six perfections form one inseparable whole, and the larger Sutras devote a considerable amount of space to detailed surveys of all the six Paramitas.

1. RELATION OF PERFECT WISDOM TO THE OTHER PERFECTIONS

35.

The Lord : It is from the great ocean of the perfection of wisdom that the great jewel of the all-knowledge of the Tathagatas has come forth.

Ananda : The Lord does not praise the perfection of giving, nor any of the first five perfections ; he does not proclaim their name. Only the perfection of wisdom does the Lord praise, its name alone he proclaims.

The Lord : So it is, Ananda. For the perfection of wisdom controls the five perfections. What do you think, Ananda, can giving undedicated to all-knowledge be called perfect giving ?

Ananda : No, Lord.

The Lord : The same is true of the other perfections. What do you think, Ananda, is that wisdom inconceivable which turns over the wholesome roots by dedicating them to all-knowledge ?

Ananda : Yes, it is inconceivable, completely inconceivable.

The Lord : The perfection (pāramitā) of wisdom therefore gets its name from its supreme excellence (paramatvāt). Through it the wholesome roots, dedicated to all-knowledge, get the name of "perfections". It is therefore because it has dedicated the wholesome roots to all-knowledge that the perfection of wisdom controls, guides and leads the five perfections. The five perfections are in this manner contained in the perfection of wisdom, and the term "perfection of wisdom" is just a synonym for the fulfilment of the six perfections. In consequence, when the perfection of wisdom is proclaimed, all the six perfections are proclaimed.

36.

Sariputra : It is just the perfection of wisdom which directs the five perfections in their ascent on the path to all-knowledge. Just as, Kausika, people born blind, 100, or 1,000, or 100,000 of them, cannot, without a leader, go along a path and get to a village, town or city ; just so, Giving, Morality, Patience, Vigour and Trance cannot by themselves be called "perfections", for without the perfection of wisdom they are as if born blind, without their leader unable to ascend the path to all-knowledge, and still less can they reach all-knowledge. When, however, Giving, Morality, Patience, Vigour and Trance are taken hold of by the perfection of wisdom, then they are termed "perfections", for then these five perfections acquire an organ of vision which allows them to ascend the path to all-knowledge, and to reach all-knowledge.

37.

The Lord : When a Bodhisattva trains in the perfection of wisdom, all the perfections are automatically incorporated, taken up, followed after, and included. The view of individuality includes all the sixty-two views, and even so, for a Bodhisattva who trains in the perfection of wisdom, all the perfections are included in that. As long as someone's life-faculty goes on, all the other faculties are included in it. Even so for a Bodhisattva who trains in perfect wisdom all the other perfections are included in that. When someone's life-faculty is stopped, all the other faculties are also stopped. Even so, for a Bodhisattva who trains in perfect wisdom, all the other unwholesome dharmas are stopped when only non-cognition is stopped, and all the other perfections are included in that, and automatically taken hold of.

38.

The Lord: The perfection of wisdom, in particular, should be regarded as the Bodhisattva's good friend. All the six perfections, in fact, are the good friends of a Bodhisattva. They are his Teacher, his path, his light, his torch, his illumination, his shelter, his refuge, his place of rest, his final relief, his island, his mother, his father, and they lead him to cognition, to understanding, to full enlightenment. For it is in these six perfections that the perfection of wisdom is accomplished. Simply from the six perfections has come forth the all-knowledge of the Tathagatas who, in the past period, have won full enlightenment and then entered Nirvana. And so has the all-knowledge of the Tathagatas of the future period, and so has the all-knowledge of the Tathagatas who just now reside in incalculable, immeasurable, infinite and inconceivable world-systems. I also, Subhuti, am a Tathagata who has in this present period won full enlightenment, and my all-knowledge also has come forth from the six perfections. For the six perfections contain the thirty-seven dharmas which act as the wings to enlightenment, they contain the four Brahma-dwellings, the four means of conversion, and any Buddha-dharma there may be, any Buddha-cognition, cognition of the Self-Existent, any unthinkable, incomparable, immeasurable, incalculable, unequalled .cognition, any cognition which equals the unequalled, any cognition of the all-knowing. Therefore, Subhuti, simply the six perfections of a Bodhisattva should be known as his good friends. In addition, a Bodhisattva who trains in the six perfections becomes a true benefactor to all beings who are in need of one. But if he wants to train in the six perfections, a Bodhisattva must above all hear this perfection of wisdom, take it up, bear it in mind, recite, study, spread, demonstrate, expound, explain and write it, and investigate its meaning, content and method, meditate on it, and ask questions about it. For this perfection of wisdom directs the six perfections, guides, leads, instructs and advises them, is their genetrix and nurse. Because, if they are deprived of the perfection of wisdom, the first five perfections do not come under the concept of "perfections", and they do not deserve to be called "perfections". A Bodhisattva should therefore train in just this perfection of wisdom if he wants to get to a state where he cannot be led astray by others, and to stand firmly in it.

2. THE SIX PERFECTIONS COLLECTIVELY

39.

Sakra : Those persons who hear, study, spread and write this deep perfection of wisdom surpass those Bodhisattvas who are great almsgivers, but lack in perfect wisdom and skill in

means ; and equally those whose morality is perfectly pure,
who possess a vast quantity of morality, whose observation
of the moral rules is unbroken, flawless, unstained, complete,
perfectly pure and unspotted, but who lack in perfect wisdom
and skill in means ; and equally those who have won patience,
and peaceful calm, whose thoughts are free from hostility, who
feel no thought of malice even when burned at the stake, but
who lack in perfect wisdom and skill in means ; and equally
those who have exerted vigour, who persist in trying, who are
free from sloth, and remain uncowed in all they do with body,
voice and mind, but who lack in perfect wisdom and skill in
means ; and equally those who are fond of the trances, and
delight in them, who are strong and powerful in the trances,
who are established in the trances, who are masters of the
trances, but who lack in perfect wisdom and skill in means.

40.

Subhuti : What is a Bodhisattva's perfection of giving ?
The Lord : Here a Bodhisattva, his thoughts associated
with the knowledge of all modes, gives gifts, i.e. inward or
outward things, and, having made them common to all beings,
he dedicates them to supreme enlightenment ; and also others
he instigates thereto. But there is nowhere an apprehension
of anything.
Subhuti : What is a Bodhisattva's perfection of morality ?
The Lord : He himself lives under the obligation of the ten
ways of wholesome acting, and also others he instigates thereto.
Subhuti : What is a Bodhisattva's perfection of patience ?
The Lord : He himself becomes one who has achieved
patience, and others also he instigates to patience.
Subhuti : What is a Bodhisattva's perfection of vigour ?
The Lord : He dwells persistently in the five perfections,
and also others he instigates to do likewise.
Subhuti : What is the Bodhisattva's perfection of concen-
tration (or meditation) ?
The Lord : He himself, through skill in means, enters into
the trances, yet he is not reborn in the corresponding heavens
of form as he could ; and others also he instigates to do
likewise.
Subhuti : What is a Bodhisattva's perfection of wisdom ?
The Lord : He does not settle down in any dharma, he

contemplates the essential original nature of all dharmas ; and others also he instigates to the contemplation of all dharmas.

41.

Sariputra : How should a Bodhisattva make endeavours in the perfection of wisdom ?

The Lord : Here, Sariputra, a Bodhisattva has stood in the perfection of wisdom, by way of not taking his stand on it, and he should perfect the perfection of giving, by way of non-renunciation, because gift, giver and recipient have not been apprehended. He should fulfil the perfection of morality, on account of the fact that he transgresses into neither offence nor no-offence. He should fulfil the perfection of patience, through his imperturbability. He should fulfil the perfection of vigour, through the indefatigability of his physical and mental energy. He should fulfil the perfection of concentrated meditation, by the fact that he does not enjoy the state of trance. He should fulfil the perfection of wisdom, through the fact that neither wisdom nor stupidity are taken up.

3.   The Six Perfections Singly

(a) The perfection of giving :
42.

Sariputra : What is the worldly, and what is the supra-mundane perfection of giving ?

Subhuti : The worldly perfection of giving consists in this : The Bodhisattva gives liberally to all those who ask, all the while thinking in terms of real things.[1] It occurs to him : "I give, that one receives, this is the gift. I renounce all my possessions without stint. I act as the Buddha commands. I practise the perfection of giving. I, having made this gift into the common property of all beings, dedicate it to supreme enlightenment, and that without apprehending anything. By means of this gift and its fruit, may all beings in this very life be at their ease, and may they one day enter Nirvana !" Tied by three ties he gives a gift. Which three ? A perception of self, a perception of others, a perception of the gift.

The supramundane perfection of giving, on the other hand, consists in the threefold purity. What is the threefold purity ?

---

[1] Literally : leaning on something.

Here a Bodhisattva gives a gift, and he does not apprehend a self, a recipient, a gift ; also no reward of his giving. He surrenders that gift to all beings, but he apprehends neither beings nor self. He dedicates that gift to supreme enlightenment, but he does not apprehend any enlightenment. This is called the supramundane perfection of giving.

(b) The Perfection of morality.

43.

The Lord : An irreversible Bodhisattva observes the ten ways of wholesome action. He himself observes, and he instigates others to observe, abstention from taking life, abstention from taking what is not given, abstention from wrong conduct as regards sensuous pleasures, abstention from intoxicants as tending to cloud the mind, abstention from lying speech, abstention from malicious speech, abstention from harsh speech, abstention from indistinct prattling, abstention from covetousness, abstention from ill-will, abstention from wrong views. Even in his dreams he never commits offences against those ten precepts, and he does not nurse such offences in his mind. Even in his dreams an irreversible Bodhisattva keeps the ten wholesome paths of action present in his mind.

44.

The Lord : A Bodhisattva progresses to perfect purity of morality, i.e. he pays no attention to the ideas of the Disciples or Pratyekabuddhas, nor to any other dharmas which make for bad behaviour or which could cause delays on the road to enlightenment.

(c) The Perfection of Patience.

45.

The Lord : A Bodhisattva is firmly grounded in the power of patience when his attitude towards all beings is free from ill-will and a desire to harm them.

46.

The Lord : A Tathagata's perfection of patience is really no perfection. Because, Subhuti, when the king of Kalinga cut my flesh from every limb, at that time I had no notion of a self, or of a being, or of a soul, or of a person, nor had I any notion or non-notion. And why ? If, Subhuti, at that time I had had a notion of self, I would also have had a notion of ill-will at that time. If I had had a notion of a being, of a soul, of a person, then I also would have had a notion of ill-will at that time. And why ? By my superknowledge I know the past, five hundred births, and how I have been the Rishi, "Preacher of Patience". Then also I have had no notion of a self, or a being, or a soul, or a person. Therefore then, Subhuti, a Bodhisattva, a great being should, after he has got rid of all notions, raise his thought to the supreme enlightenment. Unsupported by form a thought should be produced, un-supported by sounds, smells, tastes, touchables or mind-objects a thought should be produced, unsupported by dharma a thought should be produced, unsupported by no-dharma a thought should be produced, unsupported by anything a thought should be produced. And why ? What is supported has no support.

(d) The Perfection of Vigour

47.

Purna : Here a Bodhisattva, who courses towards enlighten-ment and who has stood in the perfection of giving, gives gifts, not for the sake of a limited number of beings, but, on the contrary, for the sake of all beings. And so for the other perfections. When a Bodhisattva puts on the great armour, he does not circumscribe beings and say, "so many beings I will lead to Nirvana, so many beings I will not lead to Nirvana ; so many beings will I introduce to enlightenment, so many beings I will not introduce to enlightenment". But, on the contrary, it is for the sake of all beings that he puts on the great armour, and he reflects : "I myself, I will fulfil the perfection of giving, and also on all beings will I enjoin the perfection of giving". And so for the other perfections.

(e) The Perfection of Concentration

48.

Purna : If a Bodhisattva, although he enters the trances, the Unlimited, the formless attainments, does not gain rebirth through them, does not even relish them, is not captivated by them, that is his perfection of concentration.

49.

The Lord : When he practises the perfection of meditation for the sake of other beings his mind becomes undistracted. For he reflects that "even worldly meditation is hard to accomplish with distracted thoughts, how much more so is full enlightenment.   Therefore I must remain undistracted until I have won full enlightenment". . . . Moreover, Subhuti, a Bodhisattva, beginning with the first thought of enlightenment, practises the perfection of meditation.   His mental activities are associated with the knowledge of all modes when he enters into meditation.   When he has seen forms with his eye, he does not seize upon them as signs of realities which concern him, nor is he interested in the accessory details.   He sets himself to restrain that which, if he does not restrain his organ of sight, might give occasion for covetousness, sadness or other evil and unwholesome dharmas to reach his heart.   He watches over the organ of sight.   And the same with the other five sense-organs,—ear, nose, tongue, body, mind.

Whether he walks or stands, sits or lies down, talks or remains silent, his concentration does not leave him.   He does not fidget with his hands or feet, or twitch his face ; he is not incoherent in his speech, confused in his senses, exalted or uplifted, fickle or idle, agitated in body or mind.   Calm is his body, calm is his voice, calm is his mind.   His demeanour shows contentment, both in private and public. . . . He is frugal, easy to feed, easy to serve, of good life and habits ; though in a crowd he dwells apart ; even and unchanged, in gain and loss ; not elated, not cast down.   Thus in happiness and suffering, in praise and blame, in fame and disrepute, in life or death, he is the same unchanged, neither elated nor cast down.   And so with foe or friend, with what is pleasant or unpleasant, with holy or unholy men, with noises or music, with forms that are dear or undear, he remains the same unchanged, neither elated nor cast down, neither gratified nor thwarted.   And why ? Because he sees all dharmas as empty of marks of their own, without true reality, incomplete and uncreated.

(f) The Perfection of Wisdom

50.

Subhuti : What is the supramundane perfection of wisdom ? Through the fact that neither self, nor being, nor gift, nor enlightenment have been apprehended, and through the three-fold purity, he cleanses the perfection of giving for the sake of enlightenment. Through the fact that neither self nor being nor morality nor enlightenment have been apprehended, he cleanses the perfection of morality for the sake of enlightenment. And so with the other perfections. For the sake of enlightenment he dedicates all wholesome roots to the supreme enlightenment, by means of an undifferentiated dedication, by means of a dedication which is supreme, which equals the unequalled, which is unthinkable, incomparable and measureless. This is called the supramundane perfection of wisdom.

III.   THE ELUSIVENESS OF PERFECT WISDOM

51.

Subhuti : Deep is the essential original nature of dharmas.

The Lord : Because it is isolated.

Subhuti : Deep is the essential nature of perfect wisdom.

The Lord : Because its essential nature is pure and isolated.

Subhuti : Isolated in its essential nature is the perfection of wisdom. I pay homage to the perfection of wisdom !

The Lord : Also all dharmas are isolated in their essential nature. And the isolation of the essential nature of all dharmas is identical with the perfection of wisdom. For the Tathagata has fully known all dharmas as not made.

Subhuti : Therefore all dharmas have the character of not having been fully known by the Tathagata ?

The Lord : It is just through their essential nature that those dharmas are not a something. Their nature is no-nature, and their no-nature is their nature. Because all dharmas have one mark only, i.e. no mark. It is for this reason that all dharmas have the character of not having been fully known by the Tathagata. For there are not two natures of dharma, but just one single one is the nature of all dharmas. And the nature of all dharmas is no nature, and their no-nature is their nature. It is thus that all points of attachment are abandoned.

Subhuti : Deep, O Lord, is the perfection of wisdom !

The Lord : Through a depth like that of space.

Subhuti : Hard to understand, O Lord, is the perfection of wisdom!

The Lord : Because nothing is fully known by the enlightened.

Subhuti : Unthinkable, O Lord, is the perfection of wisdom !

The Lord : Because the perfection of wisdom is not something that thought ought to know, or that thought has access to.

Subhuti : Not something made is the perfection of wisdom, O Lord!

The Lord : Because no maker can be apprehended.

Subhuti : How then, under these circumstances, should a Bodhisattva course in perfect wisdom ?

The Lord : A Bodhisattva courses in perfect wisdom, if, while coursing, he does not course in the skandhas ; or if he does not course in the conviction that the skandhas are impermanent, or that they are empty, or that they are either defective or entire. And if he does not even course in the conviction that form is not the defectiveness or entirety of form, and so for the other skandhas, then he courses in perfect wisdom.

Subhuti : It is wonderful, O Lord, how well the reasons for the attachment and non-attachment of the Bodhisattvas have been explained.

The Lord : One courses in perfect wisdom if one does not course in the idea that form is with attachment, or without attachment. And as for form, so for the other skandhas ; for the sight-organ, etc. to, feeling born from eye-contact ; for the physical elements, the six perfections, the thirty-seven wings of enlightenment, the powers, the grounds of self-confidence, the analytical knowledges, the eighteen special Buddha-dharmas and the fruits of the holy life, from the fruit of a Streamwinner to all-knowledge. When he courses thus, a Bodhisattva does not generate attachment to anything, from form to all-knowledge. For all-knowledge is unattached, and it is neither bound nor freed, and there is nothing that has risen above it. It is thus, Subhuti, that Bodhisattvas should course in perfect wisdom through rising completely above all attachments.

Subhuti : It is wonderful, O Lord, how deep is this dharma, I mean the perfection of wisdom. Demonstration does not diminish or increase it. Non-demonstration also does not diminish or increase it.

The Lord : Well said, Subhuti. It is just as if a Tathagata should, during his entire life, speak in praise of space, without thereby increasing the volume of space ; and space would not diminish, either, while he was not speaking in praise of it. Or it is as with an illusory man. Praise does not penetrate into him or win him over. When there is no praise, he is not affected or frustrated. Just so the true nature of dharma is just so much, whether it be demonstrated or not.

Subhuti : A doer of what is hard is the Bodhisattva who, while he courses in perfect wisdom, does not lose heart nor get elated ; who persists in making endeavours about it, and does not turn back. The development of perfect wisdom is like the development of space. Homage should be paid to those Bodhisattvas who are armed with this armour. For with space they want to be armed when, for the sake of beings, they put on the armour. Armed with the great armour is a Bodhisattva, a hero is a Bodhisattva, when he wants to be armed with an armour, and win full enlightenment, for the sake of beings who are like space, who are like the realm of Dharma. He is one who wants to liberate space, he is one who wants to get rid of space, he is one who has won the armour of the great perfection of vigour, that Bodhisattva who is armed with the armour for the sake of beings who are like space, who are like the realm of Dharma.

Thereupon a certain monk saluted the Lord with folded hands and said to the Lord: I pay homage, O Lord, to the perfection of wisdom! For it neither produces nor stops any dharma.

Sakra : If someone, holy Subhuti, would make efforts about this perfection of wisdom, what would his efforts be about ?

Subhuti : He would make efforts about space. And he would make his efforts with reference to a mere vacuity if he would decide to train in perfect wisdom and to work on it.

52.

Sariputra : When the perfection of wisdom has been consummated, what dharma does it procure ?

The Lord : When consummated, the perfection of wisdom does not procure any dharma, and in consequence of that fact it comes to be styled "perfection of wisdom".

Sakra : Then, O Lord, this perfection of wisdom does not even procure all-knowledge ?

The Lord : It does not procure it as if it were a basis, or a mental process, or a volitional act.

Sakra : How then does it procure ?

The Lord : Insofar as it does not procure, to that extent it procures.

Sakra : It is wonderful, O Lord, to see the extent to which this perfection of wisdom neither produces nor stops any dharma. For the purpose of the non-production and of the non-stopping of all dharmas has the perfection of wisdom been set up, without, however, being really present.

Subhuti : Is it at all possible, O Lord, to hear the perfection of wisdom, to distinguish and consider her, to make statements and to reflect about her ? Can one explain, or learn, that because of certain attributes, tokens or signs this is the perfection of wisdom, or that here this is the perfection of wisdom, or that there that is the perfection of wisdom ?

The Lord : No indeed, Subhuti. This perfection of wisdom cannot be expounded, or learnt, or distinguished, or considered, or stated, or reflected upon by means of the skandhas, or by means of the elements, or by means of the sense-fields. This is a consequence of the fact that all Dharmas are isolated, absolutely isolated. Nor can the perfection of wisdom be understood otherwise than by the skandhas, elements or sense-fields. For just the very skandhas, elements and sense-fields are empty, isolated and calmly quiet. It is thus that the perfection of wisdom and the skandhas, elements and sense-fields are not two, nor divided. As a result of their emptiness, isolatedness and quietude they cannot be apprehended. The lack of a basis of apprehension in all Dharmas, that is called "perfect wisdom". Where there is no perception, appellation, conception or conventional expression, there one speaks of "perfect wisdom".

53.

Subhuti : When one speaks of a "Bodhisattva", what dharma does the word "Bodhisattva" denote ? I do not, O Lord, see that dharma "Bodhisattva", nor a dharma called "perfect wisdom". Since I neither find, apprehend, nor see a dharma "Bodhisattva", nor a "perfect wisdom", what Bodhisattva shall I instruct and admonish in what perfect wisdom ? And yet, O Lord, if, when this is pointed out, a Bodhisattva's heart does not become cowed, nor stolid, does not despair nor despond, if he does not turn away, or become dejected, does not tremble, is not frightened or terrified, it is just this Bodhisattva, this great being, who should be instructed in perfect wisdom. It is precisely this that should be recognized as the perfect wisdom of that Bodhisattva, as his instruction in perfect wisdom. When he thus stands firm, that is his instruction and admonition.

IV. THE OBJECT OF PERFECT WISDOM

1. GENERAL OUTLINE

When viewed in perfect wisdom, the world, and all that it may contain, is viewed as emptiness. A good survey of the world-view of the Prajñāpāramitā is given in the Hridaya Sutra (No. 54), which is one of the finest and most profound spiritual documents of mankind. This text is supplemented by a description of the practices of a Bodhisattva on the seventh stage of his career (No. 55), the stage on which he obtains a full understanding of the tenets of perfect wisdom.

54.

Homage to the Perfection of Wisdom, the lovely, the holy ! Avalokita, the holy Lord and Bodhisattva, was moving in the deep course of the wisdom which has gone beyond. He looked down from on high ; he beheld but five heaps ; and he saw that in their own being they were empty. Here, O Sariputra, form is emptiness and the very emptiness is form ; emptiness does not differ from form, nor does form differ from emptiness ; whatever is form, that is emptiness, whatever is emptiness, that is form. The same is true of feelings, perceptions, impulses and consciousness. Here, O Sariputra, all dharmas are marked with emptiness, they are neither produced nor stopped, neither defiled nor immaculate, neither deficient nor complete. Therefore, O Sariputra, where there is emptiness there is neither form, nor feeling, nor perception, nor impulse, nor consciousness ; no eye, or ear, or nose, or tongue, or body, or mind, ; no form, nor sound, nor smell, nor taste, nor touchable, nor object of mind ; no sight-organ element, and so forth, until we come to : no mind-consciousness element ; there is no ignorance, nor extinction of ignorance, and so forth, until we come to, there is no decay and death, no extinction of decay and death ; there is no suffering, nor origination, nor stopping, nor path ; there is no cognition, no attainment and no non-attainment.

Therefore, O Sariputra, owing to a Bodhisattva's indifference to any kind of personal attainment, and through his having relied on the perfection of wisdom, he dwells without thought-coverings. In the absence of thought-coverings he has not been made to tremble, he has overcome what can upset, in the end sustained by Nirvana. All those who appear as Buddhas in the three periods of time,—they all fully awake to the utmost, right and perfect enlightenment because they have relied on the perfection of wisdom. Therefore one should know the Prajñāpāramitā as the great spell, the spell of great knowledge, the utmost spell, the unequalled spell, allayer of all suffering, in truth,—for what could go wrong? By the Prajñāpāramitā has this spell been delivered. It runs like this : Gone, gone, gone beyond, gone altogether beyond, O what an awakening, all hail !

55.

The Lord : On the seventh stage a Bodhisattva does not seize on a self, or a being, or a soul, or a person, because, absolutely, a self, being, soul or person do not exist. He does not seize on annihilationist views ; for all dharmas are absolutely unproduced and therefore no dharma is ever annihilated. He does not seize on eternalist views ; because dharmas are not produced, and there is neither eternity nor annihilation. He has no notion of a sign, because, absolutely, defilement does not exist. He does not form the false view of a cause, because he does not review that view. He does not settle down in skandhas, elements or sense-fields, because, absolutely they do not exist. He does not settle down in anything that belongs to the triple world ; because its own-being does not exist. He is not bent on anything that belongs to the triple world, nor does he hang on to it ; because in the triple world no entity has existence, or can be apprehended. He does not settle down in any views which regard the Buddha, the Dharma, or the Samgha as a refuge ; because it is not from taking refuge in views on the Buddha, Dharma or Samgha that there is a vision of the Buddha, Dharma or Samgha. He does not settle down in views about morality as his refuge ; because perfect purity of morality does not result from taking refuge in views on morality. The conviction that all dharmas are empty does not make him dejected : because all dharmas are empty through their own marks, and not through their emptiness. He does not obstruct emptiness, because all dharmas are empty, and emptiness does not obstruct emptiness.

He should penetrate into emptiness, through the fulfillment of the emptiness of own-marks. He should realise the signless, through non-attention to all signs. He should cognize the wishless, in that no thought proceeds in him concerning the triple world. He gains the threefold perfect purity, through the fulfilment of the ten ways of wholesome action. He has full pity and compassion towards all beings, as a result of his acquisition of the great compassion. He does not despise any being, as a result of the fulfilment of his friendliness. He has a vision of the sameness of all dharmas, for he adds nothing to them, and subtracts nothing from them. He penetrates to the really true principle, through his penetration into the one principle of all dharmas, a non-penetration. He gains the patient acceptance of non-production, by patiently accepting the fact that all dharmas are unproduced, not stopped, not put together. He has a cognition of non-production, concerning the non-production of name and form. He gains the exposition of the one single principle, i.e. there is a habitual absence of all notions of duality. He uproots the fashioning of all dharmas, through his non-discrimination of all dharmas. He turns away from views, i.e. from the views held on the level of Disciples and Pratyekabuddhas. He turns away from the defilements, by the extinction of all the defilements and of the residues relating to them. He reaches the stage where quietude and insight are in equilibrium, i.e. in the cognition of the knowledge of all modes. His mind is completely tamed, for he finds no delight in anything belonging to the triple world. His mind is completely pacified, by the drawing inwards of the six sense-faculties. His cognition is unobstructed, as a result of his acquisition of the Buddha-eye. He knows the circumstances in which it is suitable to show affection, as a result of his even-mindedness concerning what belongs to the six sense-fields. He can go to whichever realm he wishes to go to, for he can exhibit his personality in a way which suits any assembly he may be in.

2. NEGATIONS

In one sense, emptiness, as the objective counterpart to total renunciation, is the complete negation of all predicates, attributes and entities. The Sutras on perfect wisdom revel in the enumeration of such negations, and we are content here with two examples (56, 57). Emptiness, in particular, implies the absence of "beings", or separate individuals (58-60), and the absence of separate dharmas, or impersonal objects (61-63). The same idea is frequently expressed by saying that everything is "unproduced" (64, 65). All the elements of the process of salvation are equally negated. There is, to begin with, no bondage, or defilement, (66, 67), no spiritual growth (68, 69), and no attainment of emancipation (70,71). The attitude of a Bodhisattva to objects in general is defined by saying that he should not apprehend them (72), that he should not mind them (73, 74), that he should not be supported by them (75-78 ; cf. no. 46).

56.

Mañjusri : What are the qualities and what the advantages of a perfection of wisdom which is without qualities ? How can one speak of the qualities or advantages of a perfect wisdom which is incapable of doing anything, neither raises up nor destroys anything, neither accepts nor rejects any dharma, is powerless to act and not at all busy, if its own-being cannot be cognized, if its own-being cannot be seen, if it does not bestow any dharma, and does not obstruct any dharma, if it brings about the non-separateness of all dharmas, does not exalt the single oneness of all dharmas, does not effect the

separateness of all dharmas, if it is not made, not something
to be done, not passed, if it does not destroy anything, if it is
not a donor of the dharmas of the common people, of the
dharmas of the Arhats, of the dharmas of the Pratyekabuddhas,
of the dharmas of the Bodhisattvas, and not even of the dharmas
of a Buddha, and does not take them away, if it does not toil
in birth-and-death, nor cease toiling in Nirvana, neither
bestows nor destroys the dharmas of a Buddha, if it is unthinkable and inconceivable, not something to be done, not something to be undone, if it neither produces nor stops any dharmas,
neither annihilates them nor makes them eternal, if it neither
causes to come nor to go, brings about neither detachment
nor non-detachment, neither duality nor non-duality, and if,
finally, it is non-existent ?

The Lord : Well have you, Mañjusri, described the qualities
of perfect wisdom. But nevertheless a Bodhisattva should
train in just this perfection of wisdom, in the manner of no-
training, if he wants to train in, and to accomplish, that concentration of a Bodhisattva which allows him to see all the
Buddhas, the Lords, if he wants to see their Buddha-fields, and
to know their names, and if he wants to perfect the supreme
worship of those Buddhas and Lords, and firmly to believe in
and to fathom their demonstration of dharma.

Mañjusri : For what reason is this the perfection of wisdom ?

The Lord : It is called "perfect wisdom" because it is neither
produced nor stopped. And it is so because it is calmly quiet
from the very beginning, because there is no escape, because
there is nothing to be accomplished, and, finally, because of its
non-existence. For what is non-existence, that is perfect
wisdom. It is for this reason that one should expect Bodhisattvas
to develop perfect wisdom. It is the range of the Bodhisattvas,
—the great beings,—ranging in all dharmas.

57.

The Lord : This, Kausika, is the meaning of the perfection
of wisdom : The perfection of wisdom should not be viewed
from duality nor from non-duality ; not from a sign nor from
the signless ; not through bestowal nor through withdrawal ;
not through subtracting something nor through adding something ; not from defilement nor from non-defilement ; not
from purification, nor from non-purification ; not through

abandoning nor through non-abandoning ; not from taking
one's stand nor from not taking one's stand ; not through
junction nor through no-junction ; not through a connection
nor through a non-connection ; not through a condition nor
through a non-condition ; not from dharma nor from no-
dharma ; not from Suchness nor from no-Suchness ; not from
the reality-limit nor from the no-reality-limit.

58.

The Lord : Here, Subhuti, one who has set out on the career
of a Bodhisattva should reflect in such a wise : "As many
beings as there are in the universe of beings, comprehended
under the term "beings",—egg-born, or born from a womb, or
moisture born, or miraculously born, with or without form,
with perception, without perception, with neither perception
nor non-perception,—as far as any conceivable universe of
beings is conceived ; all these I should lead to Nirvana, into
the realm of Nirvana which leaves nothing behind. But,
although innumerable beings have thus been led to Nirvana,
no being at all has been led to Nirvana. And why ? If in a
Bodhisattva the perception of a "being" should take place he
would not be called a "Bodhi-being". He is not to be called a
"Bodhi-being", in whom the perception of a self should take
place, or the perception of a being, or the perception of a living
soul, or the perception of a person.

59.

The Lord : A Bodhisattva, Subhuti, should carry out such a
renunciation of a gift for the weal of all beings. For that
which is the perception of being, that is yet no perception.
Those all-beings, of whom the Tathagata has spoken, they are
indeed no-beings. Because the Tathagata speaks in accordance
with reality, speaks the truth, speaks thus and not otherwise.
A Tathagata does not speak falsely.

60.

The Lord : "Perfect wisdom" and "Bodhisattva", mere
words are these. And the reality which corresponds to the
word "Bodhisattva" cannot be apprehended, either inwardly
or outwardly, or between both. It is well known that one
speaks of a living "being" although no such thing can be

apprehended in actual reality ; and that word "being" is a mere concept, is a conceptual dharma, has the status of a concept ; except insofar as it is conventionally expressed by means of a mere conventional term, there is no production or stopping of this conceptual dharma. In the same way, that which corresponds in reality to such words as "perfect wisdom", or "Bodhisattva", that is a mere conceptual dharma ; it is neither produced nor stopped, except for the conventional expression by means of a mere conventional term. . . . A dream, an echo, a mirage, a reflected image, a mock show, a magical creation of the Tathagata, all these are conceptual dharmas, and of these conceptual dharmas there is no production, nor stopping, except insofar as they are conventionally expressed by means of mere conceptual terms. Just so "perfect wisdom" and "Bodhisattva" are just conceptual dharmas, and they are neither produced nor stopped except insofar as they are conventionally expressed by means of mere conceptual terms.

61.

Sariputra : What is the perfectly pure Wisdom Eye of the Bodhisattva, the great being ?

The Lord : A Bodhisattva who is endowed with that Wisdom Eye does not wisely know any dharma,—be it conditioned or unconditioned, wholesome or unwholesome, faulty or faultless, with or without outflows, defiled or undefiled, worldly or supramundane. With that Wisdom Eye he does not see any dharma, nor learn of one, nor know one, nor discern one.

62.

The Lord : Someone who has set out in the Bodhisattva-vehicle should know, see, and resolve upon all dharmas in such a way that he has nothing to do with either the notion of a dharma, or the notion of a no-dharma. And why ? "Notion of dharma, notion of dharma", O Subhuti, as no-notion has that been taught by the Tathagata. Therefore is it called "notion of dharma".

63.

The Lord : Bodhisattvas, great beings have no notion of a dharma, Subhuti, nor a notion of non-dharma. They have no notion or non-notion at all. For if these Bodhisattvas should have the notion of a dharma, then they would thereby seize on a self, on a being, on a soul, on a person. A Bodhisattva should therefore certainly not take up a dharma, nor a non-dharma. Therefore this saying has been taught by the Tathagata in a hidden sense : "Those who know the discourse on dharma as a raft should forsake dharmas, and how much more so non-dharmas".

64.

The Lord : Do you then, Subhuti, see a real dharma which courses in perfect wisdom ?

Subhuti : No, Lord.

The Lord : Do you see that perfect wisdom, in which the Bodhisattva courses, as a real thing ?

Subhuti : No, Lord.

The Lord : Do you see as real that dharma which offers no basis for apprehension ? Has that dharma by any chance been produced, or will it be produced, or is it being produced; has it been stopped, will it be stopped, or is it being stopped ?

Subhuti : No, Lord.

The Lord : This insight gives a Bodhisattva the patient acceptance of dharmas which fail to be produced. When he is endowed with that, he is predestined to full enlightenment. He is bound to progress towards the self-confidence of a Tathagata. It is quite impossible that a Bodhisattva who courses, strives and struggles in this way, and progresses in this direction, should not reach the supreme cognition of a Buddha, the cognition of the all-knowing, the cognition of the great Caravan Leader.

65.

Subhuti : "Bodhisattva", a mere designation is that. It has the same degree of reality as the self. One speaks of a "self", but absolutely the self is something uncreated. Since thus all dharmas have no own-being, what is that form, which is something uncreated ? And so for the other skandhas. But what is uncreated, that is not form, or feeling, or perception, or impulse, or consciousness. How shall I instruct and admonish a non-creation in a perfection of wisdom which is also a non-creation ? And yet, one cannot apprehend as other than uncreated (the dharmas of) a Bodhisattva who lives for the sake of enlightenment. . . . A Bodhisattva, who courses in perfect wisdom, does not review a non-creation as one thing, and a Bodhisattva as another. A Bodhisattva and a non-creation are not two or divided. Nor does he review form, etc., as other than a non-creation. For a non-creation and all dharmas are not two or divided. If, when this is being expounded, the heart of a Bodhisattva is not cowed, nor becomes stolid, or regretful, and if his mind does not tremble, is not frightened nor terrified, then such a Bodhisattva courses in perfect wisdom. For he reviews all dharmas as without inward striving, as similar to a mock show, a dream, a mirage, an echo, an image, a reflection of the moon in the water, a magical creation, a village of the Gandharvas.

66.

Subhuti : How is perfect wisdom marked ?

The Lord : It is marked with the non-attachment of space. It is, however, no mark, nor does it have one.

Subhuti : Would it be possible for all dharmas to be found by the same mark by which the perfection of wisdom is to be found ?

The Lord : So it is, Subhuti, so it is. The mark by which perfect wisdom exists, through just that mark all dharmas also exist. Because all dharmas are isolated in their own-being, empty in their own-being. In that way all dharmas exist through the mark by which perfect wisdom exists, i.e. through the mark of emptiness, through the mark of isolation.

Subhuti : If all dharmas are isolated from all dharmas, if all dharmas are empty of all dharmas, how can one then conceive of the defilement and purification of beings ? Because what is isolated, that is neither defiled nor purified. Emptiness also is neither defiled nor purified. Neither the isolated, nor emptiness can fully know the supreme enlightenment. The isolated does not apprehend any dharma in emptiness. The isolated does not apprehend in emptiness any being that can know full enlightenment. How shall we understand the meaning of this teaching, O Lord ?

The Lord : What do you think, Subhuti, do beings indulge for a long time in I-making and mine-making ?

Subhuti : They do, O Lord.

The Lord: Are, then, I-making and mine-making isolated and empty ?

Subhuti : They are, O Lord.

The Lord : Is it because of I-making and mine-making that beings run and wander about in birth-and-death?

Subhuti : Yes, so it is, O Lord.

The Lord : It is surely in this sense that one conceives of beings as defiled. Insofar as they indulge in I-making and mine-making, insofar as they take hold of things,—they are defiled. Insofar, however, as they do not take hold of things, insofar they are considered as purified, and do not run about and wander in birth-and-death.

67.

Purna, son of Maitrayani : You say, Subhuti, that form, feeling, etc., are neither bound nor freed ?

Subhuti : So I do, Purna.

Purna : What is that form, etc., which is neither bound nor freed ?

Subhuti : That form which is like a dream, or an echo, a mock show, a mirage, a reflection in the water, an apparition, that form is neither bound nor freed. And so for the other skandhas. Past, future and present form, etc., is neither bound nor freed, whether it be wholesome or unwholesome, defiled or undefiled, tainted or untainted, with or without outflows, worldly or supramundane. Because it has no being, is isolated, calmly quiet, empty, signless, wishless, has not been brought together, has not been produced. And what is true of form, that is true of the other skandhas, and of all dharmas. Neither bound nor freed a Bodhisattva will win a knowledge of all modes which is neither bound nor freed, turn a wheel of dharma which is neither bound nor freed, and he will lead, by means of the three vehicles, to Nirvana beings who are neither bound nor freed. It is thus that a Bodhisattva, through the six perfections, will, himself neither bound nor freed, fully know all dharmas, through the fact that they have no being, and that everything is isolated, calmly quiet, empty, signless, wishless, not brought together, not produced. It is thus that one should know the armour of the Bodhisattva, the great being, who is neither bound nor freed.

68.

The Lord : At the time when you, Mañjusri, develop the perfection of wisdom, which wholesome root of yours does at time accumulate or decrease ?

Mañjusri : None, O Lord.   One to whom the accumulation or decrease of any dharma whatsoever happens, he does not develop perfect wisdom.   That should not be known as a development of perfect wisdom where any accumulation or decrease of any dharma whatsoever is set up.   That, O Lord, is a development of perfect wisdom, where one neither forsakes the dharmas of an ordinary person, nor grasps at the dharmas of a Buddha.   Because the development of perfect wisdom is not set up by ṭaking as one's basis any dharma which one could forsake or grasp at.   That, O Lord, is a development of perfect wisdom, when one neither approaches the faults of birth-and-death nor longs for the virtues of Nirvana.   For one does not review birth-and-death, how much less its faults.   And I do not apprehend Nirvana, how much less will I see its virtues. That, O Lord, is a development of perfect wisdom where one appropriates no dharma whatsoever, seizes on none, escapes from none.   That, O Lord, is a development of perfect wisdom where one apprehends the diminution of no dharma whatsoever, nor its increase.   For non-production neither diminishes nor grows.   Such is a development of perfect wisdom.   That, O Lord, is a development of perfect wisdom whereby no dharma is either produced or stopped, whereby no dharma is either depleted or repleted.   Moreover, that is a development of perfect wisdom, when one strives after neither unthinkable nor definitely tangible dharmas.   That which is striven after does not exist, he who strives does not exist, that wherewith he strives does not exist.   Such a development is set up as a development of perfect wisdom.   He does not think that "these dharmas are superior, those are inferior", he does not apprehend the dharmas which might be superior or inferior.   Thus giving himself up to the practice of the development of perfect wisdom, a son of good family does not apprehend any dharma at all. The development of perfect wisdom, O Lord, does not imagine any dharma as superior or inferior.   There is nothing superior or inferior about non-production, or about Suchness, the reality-limit, or all dharmas.   Such a development, Lord, is a development of perfect wisdom.

The Lord : Are then, Mañjusri, the Buddha-dharmas not supreme ?

Mañjusri : They are supreme (agrā), but just because they

cannot be seized upon (a-grāhyatvād). Has not the Tathagata
fully known all dharmas as empty ?

The Lord : So he has, Mañjusri.

Mañjusri : But one cannot, O Lord, conceive through
emptiness of superiority or inferiority ?

The Lord : Well said, Mañjusri, well said ! So it is,
Mañjusri, as you say.

69.

Subhuti : It is wonderful to see the extent to which the
Tathagata has demonstrated the true nature of all these
dharmas, and yet one cannot properly talk about the true
nature of all these dharmas (in the sense of predicating distinctive attributes to separate real entities). As I understand
the meaning of the Tathagata's teaching, even all dharmas
cannot be talked about in any proper sense ?

The Lord : So it is, for one cannot properly express the
emptiness of all dharmas in words.

Subhuti : Can something have growth, or diminution, if it is
beyond all distinctive words ?

The Lord : No, Subhuti.

Subhuti : But if there is no growth or diminution of an entity
which is beyond all distinctive words, then there can be no
growth or diminution of the six perfections. And how, then,
could a Bodhisattva win full enlightenment through the force
of these six perfections, if they do not grow, and how could he
come close to full enlightenment, since, without fulfilling the
perfections, he cannot come close to full enlightenment ?

The Lord : So it is, Subhuti. There is certainly no growth or
diminution of a perfection-entity. A Bodhisattva who practises
perfect wisdom, who develops perfect wisdom, and who is
skilled in means, does obviously not think that "this perfection
of giving grows, or diminishes". But he knows that "this
perfection of giving is a mere word". When he gives a gift he
dedicates to the supreme enlightenment of all beings the
mental activities, the productions of thought, the roots of
good which are involved in that act of giving. But he dedicates
them in such a way that he respects the actual reality of full
enlightenment. And he proceeds in the same way when he
takes upon himself the moral obligations, when he perfects
himself in patience, when he exerts vigour, enters into the
trances, practises perfect wisdom, develops perfect wisdom.

Subhuti : What, then, is this supreme enlightenment ? The Lord : It is Suchness. But Suchness neither grows nor diminishes. A Bodhisattva, who repeatedly and often dwells in mental activities connected with that Suchness, comes near to the supreme enlightenment, and he does not lose those mental activities again. It is certain that there can be no growth or diminution of an entity which is beyond all words, and that therefore neither the perfections, nor all dharmas, can grow or diminish. It is thus that, when he dwells in mental activities of this kind, a Bodhisattva becomes one who is near to perfect enlightenment.

70.

Subhuti : At the time, O Lord, when a Bodhisattva who courses in perfect wisdom investigates dharmas, at that time he reviews the non-production of all dharmas, from form to the Buddha-dharmas, on account of their absolute purity.

Sariputra : As I understand the meaning of the Venerable Subhuti's teaching, everything from form to Buddha-dharmas is non-production. But if that is so, then, surely a Disciple has already attained the enlightenment of a Disciple, a Pratyekabuddha that of a Pratyekabuddha, and a Bodhisattva has already attained the knowledge of all modes. There will then be no distinction of the five places of rebirth. If all dharmas are non-production, a Bodhisattva has already attained the five-fold enlightenment. For what purpose should the Stream-winner develop the path for the sake of forsaking the three fetters ; or the Once-Returner for the sake of attenuating greed, hate and delusion ; or the Never-Returner for the sake of forsaking the five lower fetters ; or the Arhat for the sake of forsaking the five higher fetters ? For what purpose does one who belongs to the vehicle of the Pratyekabuddhas develop the path for the sake of attaining the enlightenment of a Pratyeka-buddha ? For what reason does a Bodhisattva go on the difficult pilgrimage, and experience all those sufferings for the sake of beings ? For what reason has a Tathagata known full enlightenment, for what reason has he turned the wheel of dharma ?

Subhuti : I do not wish or look for the attainment of an unproduced dharma, nor for reunion with one. I do not wish for the streamwinnership of non-production, nor for the fruit of a streamwinner in non-production. I do not wish or look for any of the spiritual attainments, up to the enlightenment of a Pratyekabuddha, on the part of non-production. Nor do I wish or look for a Bodhisattva who has gone on the difficult pilgrimage. In any case, one who courses in the notion of difficulties is not a Bodhisattva. For one who has generated in himself the notion of difficulties is unable to work the weal of countless beings. On the contrary, he forms the notion that all beings are like his parents and children, that they are like himself, and then he is able to work the weal of countless beings. He also thinks that "just as one speaks of a self, and yet, absolutely, a self is unproduced, so also all inner and outer dharmas are unproduced". If he forms such a notion of all dharmas, then he will have no notion of difficulties. For a Bohisattva will in each and every way not produce any dharma nor apprehend one. I also do not wish or look for an unproduced Tathagata, nor for a full enlightenment which is non-production, nor for a turning of the wheel of dharma which is non-production. I do, in fact, not wish or look for an unproduced attainment which is being attained by an unproduced dharma. . . .

Sariputra: Is there, then, no attainment, is there no reunion?

Subhuti : There is attainment, there is reunion, but not in the ultimate sense. But it is by means of worldly conventional expressions that one conceives of attainment and reunion, of streamwinners, etc., to Buddha,—but not in the ultimate sense . . .

Sariputra: And in the same way, also, the differentiation of the five places of rebirth takes place only by way of worldly conventional expression, and in the ultimate sense it does not take place ?

Subhuti : So it is, Sariputra. Because in the ultimate sense there is neither karma nor karma-result, neither production nor stopping, neither defilement nor purification.

71.

The Lord : What do you think, Subhuti, does it occur to a Streamwinner that "I have attained the fruit of a Streamwinner ?"—Subhuti : No, Lord. Because he has not won any dharma. Therefore is he called a "Streamwinner". No form has been won, no sounds, smells, tastes, touchables, or objects of mind have been won. Therefore is he called a Streamwinner. If, O Lord, a Streamwinner should think that "I have attained the fruit of a Streamwinner," then he would thereby seize on a self, on a being, on a soul, on a person.—The Lord : Does it then occur to a Once-Returner that "I have attained the fruit of a Once-Returner ?"—Subhuti : No, Lord. For there is not any dharma that has won Once-Returnership. Therefore is he called a Once-returner.—The Lord : Does it then occur to a Never-Returner, "I have attained the fruit of a Never-Returner ?"—Subhuti : No, Lord. For there is not any dharma that has won Never-Returnership. Therefore is he called a Never-Returner.—The Lord : Does it then occur to an Arhat, "I have attained Arhatship ?"—Subhuti : No, Lord. For there is not any dharma which is called "Arhat". Therefore is he called an "Arhat". If, O Lord, an Arhat should think that "I have attained Arhatship", he would thereby seize on a self, on a being, on a soul, on a person. And why ? I am, O Lord, the one whom the Tathagata has pointed out as the foremost of those who dwell in Peace. I am, O Lord, an Arhat free from greed. And yet, O Lord, it does not occur to me that "an Arhat am I and free from greed". If, O Lord, I should think that I had attained Arhatship, then the Tathagata would not have declared of me, "The foremost of those who dwell in Peace, Subhuti, son of good family, dwells not anywhere, therefore is he called a 'dweller in Peace', 'a dweller in Peace', indeed".

72.

Subhuti : Absolutely, form, etc., does not exist and is not apprehended. How could "Bodhisattva" be a word that denotes form, etc. ?

The Lord : Well said, Subhuti. A Bodhisattva who courses in perfect wisdom does not apprehend any factual reality behind such words as form, etc., or permanence and impermanence, ease and suffering, calm and lack of calm, emptiness and non-emptiness, sign and signless, wish and wishless, etc. As you say, Subhuti, "I do not see, when reviewing it, that dharma 'Bodhisattva'." For a dharma cannot review the element of Dharma, nor can the element of Dharma review a dharma. The element of form cannot review the element of Dharma, and vice versa. The element of feeling, etc., cannot review the element of Dharma, and vice versa. The conditioned element cannot review the unconditioned element, nor can the unconditioned element review the conditioned element. One cannot make known the Unconditioned through the exclusion of the conditioned. Nor can one make known the conditioned through the exclusion of the Unconditioned. A Bodhisattva, who courses in perfect wisdom, does not review any dharma. In consequence, he is not afraid, his thought does not despondently hide in any dharma, and his mind knows no regrets. And that is because he does not review any dharma whatsoever.

Subhuti : For what reason does a Bodhisattva's heart become neither cowed nor stolid ?

The Lord : Because a Bodhisattva neither reviews nor apprehends those dharmas which constitute thought and all that belongs to it.

Subhuti : For what reason is a Bodhisattva's mind unafraid?

The Lord : A Bodhisattva does not apprehend mind or mind-element and he does not review them. It is thus that a Bodhisattva should, through the non-apprehension of all dharmas, course in perfect wisdom.

73.

The Lord: It is through absolute emptiness that Bodhisattvas, practising perfect wisdom, cleanse the road to the knowledge of all modes. Established in the perfection of giving they do not grasp at anything ; established in the perfection of morality they commit no offence ; established in the perfection of patience they remain imperturbable ; established in the perfection of vigour they are indefatigable in body and mind ; established in the perfection of concentration they know no distraction in their thoughts ; established in the perfection of wisdom they have expelled all stupid thoughts. In this way Bodhisattvas cleanse through absolute emptiness the road to the knowledge of all modes, practising perfect wisdom, and having stood in the six perfections. One conceives of giving on account of taking, of morality on account of immorality, of patience on account of impatience, of vigour on account of sloth, of concentration on account of the unconcentrated, of wisdom on account of the stupid. A Bodhisattva does not put his mind to such ideas as having crossed or not having crossed, of giver or non-giver, persons of good or bad conduct, patient or angry people, vigorous or slothful people, concentrated or unconcentrated people, wise or stupid, or to such ideas as "I am abused", "I am praised", "I am treated with respect", "I am not treated with respect". For non-production cannot put its mind to such ideas. Perfect wisdom cuts off all mindings.

74.

Sariputra: How, then, must a Bodhisattva course if he is to course in perfect wisdom?

Subhuti : He should not course in form, or in the sign of form, or in the idea "form is a sign", or in the production of form, or in the stopping or destruction of form, or in the idea that "form is empty". And so for the other skandhas. He should not entertain the idea "I course", or "I am a Bodhisattva". For the idea that he is a Bodhisattva would act as a basis. It should not occur to him that "he who courses thus, courses in perfect wisdom and develops it". He courses along, but he does not entertain such ideas as "I course", "I do not course", "I course and I do not course", "I neither course nor do not course", and the same four with "I will course". He does not go near any dharma at all, because all dharmas are unapproachable and unappropriable.

75.

The Lord : When he gives a gift, a Bodhisattva should not be supported by an entity, and he should not be supported anywhere. Not by one who is supported by form should a gift be given, nor by one who is supported by sounds, smells, tastes, touchables or mind-objects. For a Bodhisattva should give a gift as one who is not supported by the perception of a sign. And the heap of merit of a Bodhisattva, who unsupported gives a gift, is not easy to measure.

76.

The Lord : Therefore then, Subhuti, a Bodhisattva should produce an unsupported thought, a thought which is nowhere supported, which is not supported by forms, sounds, smells, tastes, touchables or objects of mind.

77.

Subhuti : Bodhisattvas do not lean on dharmas, just as all dharmas do not lean on anything.

Sariputra : How is it that all dharmas do not lean on anything?

Subhuti : Form is empty in its essential original nature. It does not lean inside, nor outside, nor can it be apprehended between both. In this manner all dharmas do not lean on anything, on account of the emptiness of their own original nature. It is thus that a Bodhisattva, who courses in the six perfections, should fully cleanse everything from form to the knowledge of all modes.

78.

Subhuti : Now, Kausika, listen and attend well. I will teach you how a Bodhisattva should stand in perfect wisdom. Through standing on emptiness should he stand in perfect wisdom. Armed with the great armour, the Bodhisattva should so develop that he does not take his stand on any of these : not on form, feeling, perception, impulses, consciousness ; not on eye, ear, nose, tongue, body, mind ; nor on forms, sounds, smells, tastes, touchables, mind-objects ; not on eye-consciousness, etc., until we come to : not on mind-consciousness ; etc., until we come to : not on mind-contact ; etc., until we come to : not on feeling from mind-contact ; not on the elements, i.e. earth, water, fire, wind, ether, consciousness ; not on the pillars of mindfulness, right efforts, roads to psychic power, faculties, powers, limbs of enlightenment, limbs of the Path ; not on the fruits of the Streamwinner, Once-Returner, Never-Returner, or Arhatship ; not on Pratyekabuddhahood, nor on Buddhahood. He should not take his stand on the ideas that "this is form", "this is feeling", etc., to "this is Buddha-hood". He should not take his stand on the ideas that "form, etc., is permanent or impermanent", that "form is ease or ill", that "form is the self or not the self", that "form is lovely or repulsive", that "form is empty or apprehended as something". He should not take his stand on the notion that the fruit of the holy life derives its dignity from the Unconditioned. Or that a Streamwinner is worthy of gifts, and will be reborn seven times, at most. Or that a Once-Returner is worthy of gifts, and will, as he has not quite won through to the end, make an end of ill after he has once more come into this world. Or that the Never-Returner is worthy of gifts, and will, without once more returning to this world, win Nirvana elsewhere. Or that an Arhat is worthy of gifts, and will just here in this very existence win Nirvana, in the realm of Nirvana that leaves nothing behind. Or that a Pratyekabuddha is worthy of gifts, and will win Nirvana after rising above the level of a Disciple, but without having attained the level of a Buddha. Or that a Buddha is worthy of gifts, and will win Nirvana, in the Buddha-Nirvana, in the realm of Nirvana that leaves nothing behind,— after he has risen above the levels of a common man, of a Disciple, and of a Pratyekabuddha, wrought the weal of countless beings, led to Nirvana countless hundreds of thousands of Niyutas of Kotis of beings, assured countless beings of Discipleship, Pratyekabuddhahood and full Buddhahood, stood on the stage of a Buddha, and done a Buddha's work,—even thereon a Bodhisattva should not take his stand.

Thereupon the Venerable Sariputra thought to himself : If even thereon he should not take his stand, how then should he stand and train himself ?

The Venerable Subhuti, through the Buddha's might, read his thoughts, and said : What do you think, Sariputra, where did the Tathagata stand ?

Sariputra : Nowhere did the Tathagata stand, because his mind sought no support. He stood neither in what is conditioned, nor in what is unconditioned, nor did he emerge from them.

Subhuti : Just so should a Bodhisattva stand, and train himself. He should decide that "as the Tathagata has not stood anywhere, nor not stood, not stood apart, nor not stood apart,—so will I stand !" "As the Tathagata is stationed, so will I stand, and train myself". "As the Tathagata is stationed, so will I stand, well placed because without a place to stand on". Even so should a Bodhisattva stand and train himself. When he trains thus, he adjusts himself to perfect wisdom, and will never cease from taking it to heart.

3. EMPTINESS

Emptiness is, however, more than the negation of all separateness. It is one of the three doors to deliverance,—i.e. Emptiness, the Signless, the Wishless—but the Sutra has nowhere dealt with this side of it in detail, except in connection with skill in means (81). It is also a term for the Absolute (79, 80). In order to facilitate meditation on emptiness, the large Prajñāpāramitā Sutra enumerates and explains twenty kinds of emptiness, I give here only the most important ones (i.e. No. 7, 8, 12-14. 16, 19) (82).

79.

The Lord : "Deep", Subhuti, is a synonym of Emptiness, of the Signless, of the Wishless, of the Uneffected, the Unproduced, of No-birth, Non-existence, Dispassion, Cessation, Nirvana, and Departing.

Subhuti : Is it a synonym only of these, or of all dharmas ?

The Lord : It is a synonym of all dharmas. For form is deep. How is form deep ? As deep as Suchness, so deep is form. As deep as the Suchness of form, so deep is form. Where there is no form, that is the depth of form. And so for the other skandhas.

Subhuti : It is wonderful, O Lord, how a subtle device has opened up form, etc., and indicated Nirvana at the same time.

80.

The Lord : The five skandhas have emptiness for own-being, and, as it is devoid of own-being, emptiness cannot crumble, cannot crumble away. It is in this sense that perfect wisdom instructs the Tathagata about this world. And as emptiness does not crumble, nor crumble away, so also the Signless, the Wishless, the Uneffected, the Unproduced, Non-existence, and the realm of Dharma.

81.

The Lord : A Bodhisattva has not abandoned all beings. He has made the special vow to set them all free. If a Bodhisattva in his mind forms the aspiration not to abandon all beings but to set them free, and if in addition he aspires for the concentration on emptiness, the signless, the wishless, i.e. for the three doors to deliverance, then that Bodhisattva should be known as one who is endowed with skill in means, and he will not realise the reality-limit midway, before his Buddha-dharmas have become complete. For it is his skill in means which protects him (from premature extinction). His thought of enlightenment consists in just that fact that he does not want to leave all beings behind. As endowed with this thought of enlightenment, and with skill in means, he does not midway realise the reality-limit. Moreover, while a Bodhisattva either actually contemplates those deep stations, i.e., the three doors to deliverance, or becomes desirous of contemplating them, he should in his mind form the following aspiration : "For a long time those beings, because they have the notion of existence, course in the apprehension of a basis. After I have won full enlightenment I shall demonstrate dharma to those beings so that they may forsake their erroneous views about a basis". As a free agent he then enters into the concentration on emptiness, on the Signless, on the Wishless. A Bodhisattva who is thus endowed with this thought of enlightenment and with skill in means does not midway realise the reality-limit. On the contrary, he does not lose his concentration on friendliness, compassion, sympathetic joy and evenmindedness. For, upheld by skill in means, he increases his pure dharmas more and more. His faith, etc., becomes keener and keener, and he acquires the powers, the limbs of enlightenment, and the path. Moreover, a Bodhisattva reflects that "for a long time those beings, because they perceive dharmas, course in the apprehension of a basis", and he develops this aspiration as he did the former one, entering the concentration on emptiness. Furthermore, he reflects that, by perceiving signs, those beings have, for a long time, coursed in signs, and he deals with this aspiration as before, entering the concentration on the Signless. Furthermore, a Bodhisattva reflects : "For a long time have these beings been perverted by the perceptions of permanence, of happiness, of the self, of loveliness. I will act in such a way that, after my full enlightenment, I shall demonstrate Dharma in order that they may forsake the perverted views of the perception of permanence, of happiness, of the self, of loveliness, and in order that they may learn that "Impermanent is all this, not permanent ; ill is all this, not happiness ; without self is all this, not with a self ; repulsive is all this, not lovely". Endowed with this thought of enlightenment, and with the previously described skill in means, taken hold of by perfect wisdom, he does not realise the reality-limit prematurely, before all his Buddha-dharmas are complete. Dwelling thus, he has entered on the concentration on the Wishless.

82.

The Lord : There is the emptiness of the Conditioned. "Conditioned" means the world of sense desire, the world of form, the formless world. The world of sense desire is empty of the world of sense desire, on account of its being neither unmoved nor destroyed. And that is its essential nature. So also for the world of form, and for the formless world.—There is the emptiness of the Unconditioned. "Unconditioned" means that of which there is neither production nor stopping, neither stability nor alteration. The Unconditioned is empty of the Unconditioned, on account of its being neither unmoved nor destroyed. And that is its essential nature.—There is the emptiness of essential nature. The essential nature of all dharmas, be they conditioned or unconditioned, is not made by Disciples, Pratyekabuddhas or Tathagatas, and it is not removed by them. Essential nature is empty of essential nature, on account of its being neither unmoved nor destroyed. And that is its essential nature.—There is the emptiness of all dharmas. "All dharmas" means : the five skandhas, the twelve sense-fields, the six kinds of consciousness, the six kinds of contact, and the six kinds of feeling conditioned by the six kinds of contact. It means conditioned dharmas and unconditioned dharmas. All dharmas are empty of all dharmas on account of their being neither unmoved nor destroyed. And that is their essential nature.—There is the emptiness of own-marks. To molest is the mark of form. To experience is the mark of feeling. To notice is the mark of perception. To fashion together is the mark of impulses. To be aware is the mark of consciousness. Whether we consider the mark of conditioned or of unconditioned dharmas, each one of all these dharmas is empty of each one of its own marks, on account of the fact that dharmas are neither unmoved nor destroyed. And that is their essential nature.—There is the emptiness of the non-existence of own-being. No dharma acting in causal connection has a being of its own, because of conditioned co-production. The causal connection is empty of the causal connection, on account of the fact that it is neither unmoved nor destroyed. And that is its essential nature.—There is the emptiness of own-being. Because own-being is the unpervertedness of essential nature, that is empty of this, on account of the fact that it is neither unmoved nor destroyed. And it is not made by either cognition or vision. For this is its essential nature.

4. MAGICAL ILLUSION

The reality character of empty dharmas is further defined by a number of similes which occur very frequently in these Sutras.
83.

Subhuti : How does a Bodhisattva come to the knowledge of the five grasping skandhas when he trains himself in the deep perfection of wisdom ?

The Lord : He comes to the knowledge of the five skandhas when he knows, according to the truth, (1) what the marks of the skandhas are, (2) how they are produced and stopped, (3) what is meant by their Suchness.

(1) Form is like a mass of foam, it has no solidity, it is full of cracks and holes, and it has no substantial inner core. Feeling is like a bubble, which swiftly rises and swiftly disappears, and it has no durable subsistence. Perception is like a mirage. As in a mirage pool absolutely no water at all can be found (so there is nothing substantial in that which is perceived). Impulses are like the trunk of a plantain tree : when you strip off one leaf-sheath after another, nothing remains, and you cannot lay hand on a core within. Consciousness is like a mock show, as when magically created soldiers, conjured up by a magician, are seen marching through the streets.

(2) The Bodhisattva wisely knows the production of the skandhas when he knows that they have come from nowhere, (although they seem to manifest themselves actually before him). He wisely knows the stopping of the skandhas when he knows that they do not go to anywhere, (although they seem to disappear altogether out of sight).

(3) The Bodhisattva perceives according to the truth that there is what is to be known as the Suchness of the five skandhas, in which there is no production or stopping, no coming or going, no defilement or purification, no growth or diminution. This Suchness is never false to its nature, and therefore is it called "Suchness". In it there is no perversion, and that is also why it is called "Suchness".

84.

The Lord : As stars, a fault of vision, as a lamp,
A mock show, dewdrops, or a bubble,
A dream, a lightning flash, or cloud,
So we should view what is conditioned.

85.

Sariputra : How should a Bodhisattva course in perfect wisdom ?

The Lord : Here a Bodhisattva, coursing in the perfection of wisdom, is truly a Bodhisattva, but he does not review a Bodhisattva, or the word "Bodhisattva", or the course of a Bodhisattva, does not review perfect wisdom, nor the word "perfect wisdom". He does not review that "he courses", nor that "he does not course". Form also he does not review, nor feeling, etc. For a Bodhisattva is empty of the own-being of a Bodhisattva, and also perfect wisdom is by its own being empty. That is its essential original nature. Because it is not through emptiness that form is empty. What is the emptiness of form that is not form. Nor is emptiness other than form. For the very form is emptiness, the very emptiness is form. Because "Bodhisattva", "perfect wisdom", "form", etc., are mere words. They are like magical illusions. Illusions and words do not stand at any point, nor on any spot. They are not, do not arise, are false to behold. For there is no production nor stopping, no defilement nor purification of something which has an own-being that is seen to be a magical illusion. A Bodhisattva who courses in perfect wisdom does therefore not review the production of a dharma, or its stopping, or its abiding, its decrease or increase, its defilement or purification. He does not review anything, from form to enlightenment, and what is called an "enlightenment-being", that also he does not review. Because words are merely artificial constructions, which do not represent dharmas. They express dharmas through adventitious designations, which are imagined and unreal. A Bodhisattva who courses in perfect wisdom does not review any realities behind those words, and, in consequence, does not settle down in them.

86.

Thereupon the thought came to some of the Gods in that

assembly : What the fairies talk and murmur, that we understand though mumbled. What Subhuti has just told us, that we do not understand ! Subhuti read their thoughts and said : There is nothing to understand, there is nothing to understand. For nothing in particular has been indicated, nothing in particular has been explained.

Thereupon the Gods thought : May the holy Subhuti enlarge on this ! May the holy Subhuti enlarge on this ! What the holy Subhuti here explores, demonstrates and teaches, that is remoter than the remote, subtler than the subtle, deeper than the deep.

Subhuti read their thoughts, and said : No one can attain any of the fruits of the holy life, or keep it,—from the Streamwinner's fruit to full enlightenment—unless he patiently accepts this elusiveness of the Dharma.

Then those Gods thought : What should one wish those to be like who are worthy to listen to the doctrine from the holy Subhuti?

Subhuti read their thoughts, and said : Those who learn the doctrine from me one should wish to be like an illusory magical creation, for they will neither hear my words, nor experience the facts which they express.

The Gods : Beings that are like a magical illusion, are they not just an illusion ?

Subhuti : Like a magical illusion are those beings, like a dream. For magical illusion and beings are not two different things, nor are dreams and beings. All objective facts (dharmas) also are like a magical illusion, like a dream. The various classes of Saints,—from Streamwinner to Buddhahood—also are like a magical illusion, like a dream.

The Gods : A fully enlightened Buddha also, you say, is like a magical illusion, is like a dream ? Buddhahood also, you say, is like a magical illusion, is like a dream ?

Subhuti : Even Nirvana, I say, is like a magical illusion, is like a dream. How much more so anything else !

The Gods : Even Nirvana, holy Subhuti, you say is like an illusion, is like a dream ?

Subhuti : Even if perchance there could be anything more distinguished, of that too I would say that it is like an illusion, like a dream. For illusion and Nirvana are not two different things, nor are dreams and Nirvana.

Thereupon the Venerable Sariputra, the Venerable Purna, son of Maitrayani, the Venerable Mahakoshthila, the Venerable Mahakatyayana, the Venerable Mahakashyapa, and the other great Disciples, together with many thousands of Bodhisattvas, said : Who Subhuti, will be those who grasp this perfection of wisdom as here explained ?

Thereupon the Venerable Ananda said to those Elders : Bodhisattvas who cannot fall back will grasp it, or persons who have reached sound views, or Arhats in whom the outflows have dried up.

Subhuti : No one will grasp this perfection of wisdom as here explained (i.e. explained in such a way that there is really no explanation at all). For no Dharma at all has been indicated, lit up, or communicated. So there will be no one who can grasp it.

87.

Subhuti : How great is that which entitles a Bodhisattva to be called "armed with the great armour ?"

The Lord : Here a Bodhisattva, a great being, thinks thus : "Countless beings I should lead to Nirvana, and yet there are none who lead to Nirvana, there are none who should be led to it." However many beings he may lead to Nirvana, yet there is not any being that has been led to Nirvana, nor that has led others to it. For such is the true nature of dharmas, seeing that their nature is illusory. Just as if, Subhuti, a clever magician, or magician's apprentice, were to conjure up at the cross roads a great crowd of people, and would make them vanish again. What do you think, Subhuti, has there anyone been killed by anyone, or murdered, or destroyed, or made to vanish ?

Subhuti : No indeed, Lord.

The Lord : Even so a Bodhisattva, a great being, leads countless beings to Nirvana, and yet there is not any being that has been led to Nirvana, nor that has led others to it. To hear this exposition without fear, that is the great thing which entitles the Bodhisattva to be known as "armed with the great armour".

Subhuti : As I understand the meaning of the Lord's teaching, as certainly not armed with an armour should this Bodhisattva, this great being, be known.

The Lord : So it is. For all-knowledge is not made, not unmade, not effected. Those beings also, for whose sake he is armed with the great armour, are not made, not unmade, not effected.

88.

The Lord : What do you think, Subhuti? Do the five grasping skandhas, after they have trained themselves in the perfection of wisdom, go forth to the knowledge of all modes ?

Subhuti : No, Lord, for the own-being of the five grasping skandhas is non-existent. The five skandhas are similar to a dream. The own-being of a dream cannot be apprehended, because it does not exist. In this way the five skandhas cannot be apprehended, because of the non-existence of their own-being.

The Lord : What do you think, Subhuti, the five skandhas which are similar to an echo, to an apparition, to a magical creation, to an image of the moon reflected in water,—do they, after they have trained themselves in perfect wisdom, go forth to the knowledge of all modes ?

Subhuti : No, Lord. For the own-being of an echo is non-existent, and so is that of an apparition, of a magical creation, of a reflected image. And thus the five skandhas cannot be apprehended, because of the non-existence of their own-being.

5. NON-DUALITY

Emptiness is also often defined as the absence of all discrimination and separateness, as non-duality, as the sameness, or identity of everything.

89.

The Lord : A Bodhisattva, Sariputra, who practises perfect wisdom produces an even state of mind towards all beings. As a result he acquires the insight into the sameness of all dharmas, and learns to establish all beings in this insight.

90.

Subhuti : What is the non-production of form, that is not form. What is the non-passing-away of form, that is not form. Thus non-production of form and form are not two nor divided. Thus the non-passing-away of form and form are not two, nor divided. Inasmuch again, as one calls anything "form", one makes a count of what is not-two. And so with feelings, etc.

91.

Subhuti : How should a Bodhisattva be trained so as to understand that "all dharmas are empty of marks of their own"?

The Lord : Form should be seen as empty of form, feeling as empty of feeling, and so forth.

Subhuti : If everything is empty of itself, how does the Bodhisattva's coursing in perfect wisdom take place ?

The Lord : A non-coursing is that coursing in perfect wisdom.

Subhuti : For what reason is it a non-coursing ?

The Lord : Because one cannot apprehend perfect wisdom, nor a Bodhisattva, nor a coursing, nor him who has coursed, nor that by which he has coursed, nor that wherein he has coursed. The coursing in perfect wisdom is therefore a non-coursing, in which all these discoursings are not apprehended.

Subhuti: How, then, should a beginner course in perfect wisdom ?

The Lord : From the first thought of enlightenment onwards a Bodhisattva should train himself in the conviction that all dharmas are baseless. While he practises the six perfections he should not take anything as a basis.

Subhuti : What makes for a basis, what for lack of basis ?

The Lord : Where there is duality, there is a basis. Where there is non-duality there is lack of basis.

Subhuti : How do duality and non-duality come about ?

The Lord : Where there is eye and forms, ear and sounds, etc., to : where there is mind and dharmas, where there is enlightenment and the enlightened, that is duality. Where there is no eye and forms, nor ear and sound, etc., to : no mind and dharmas, no enlightenment and enlightened, that is non-duality.

92.

The Lord : A development of perfect wisdom cannot take place in anyone who has the notion of existence. Because the notion of existence implies the idea "This am I", and attachment to the two extremes. But one who perceives existence and is attached to the two extremes can have no emancipation, and no development is possible in him. Because he is attached to existence.

Subhuti : What here is existence, what non-existence ?

The Lord : Duality is existence, non-duality is non-existence.

Subhuti : What here is duality, what non-duality ?

The Lord : One who perceives form, etc., has duality. One who perceives anything has duality. One who does not perceive anything has non-duality. As far as there is duality, there is existence. Insofar as there is existence, there are the karma-formations. And as far as there are karma-formations, beings are not liberated from birth, decay, sickness, death, from sorrow, lamentation, pain, sadness and despair. One who perceives duality can have none of the six perfections. Path, cognition, attainment, reunion, they are not for him. He cannot even have adaptable patience, how much less a comprehension of form, etc. How again could he have emancipation?

93.

This is the demonstration of perfect wisdom by the Bodhisattva Dharmodgata : The perfection of wisdom is self-identical, because all dharmas are the same. Perfect wisdom is isolated because all dharmas are isolated. Perfect wisdom is immobile because all dharmas are immobile. Perfect wisdom is devoid of mental acts because all dharmas are devoid of mental acts. Perfect wisdom is unbenumbed, because all dharmas are unbenumbed. Perfect wisdom has but one single taste because all dharmas have one and the same taste. Perfect wisdom is boundless because all dharmas are boundless. Perfect wisdom is non-production because all dharmas are non-production. Perfect wisdom is non-stopping because all dharmas are not stopped. As the firmament is boundless, so is perfect wisdom. As the ocean is boundless, so is perfect wisdom. As Meru shines in multi-coloured brilliance, so does the perfection of wisdom. As the firmament is not fashioned, so is perfect wisdom not fashioned. Perfect wisdom is boundless, because form and the other skandhas are boundless. Perfect wisdom is boundless because the element of earth, and the other elements, are boundless. Perfect wisdom is self-identical because the adamantine dharma is self-identical. Perfect wisdom is undifferentiated because all dharmas are undifferentiated. The non-apprehension of perfect wisdom follows from the non-apprehension of all dharmas. Perfect wisdom remains the same whatever it may surpass because all dharmas remain the same whatever they may surpass. Perfect wisdom is powerless to act because all dharmas are powerless to act. Perfect wisdom is unthinkable because all dharmas are unthinkable.

94.

Mañjusri : Perfect wisdom, O Lord, is the same as the non-production of all dharmas. It is a synonym for the inconceivable realm. But the inconceivable realm is the same as the realm of non-production, and that is the same as the realm of Dharma, and that is the same as the realm in which there are no ideas which persist by force of habit, and that again is the same as the inconceivable realm, and that is the same as the realm of self. The realm of self is thus the realm of perfect wisdom. The realm of self and the realm of perfect wisdom are not two or divided. The realm of the Tathagata and the realm of the self are not two or divided. The development of self is the development of perfect wisdom. Why that ? Perfect wisdom is a word for the realm of not-self. For one, O Lord, who would cognize the realm of not-self, he would cognize non-attachment. But when he cognizes non-attachment, he does not cognize any dharma. For the unthinkable cognition is the Buddha-cognition, the cognition of not any dharma is the Buddha-cognition.

6. CONTRADICTIONS

It has become abundantly clear, in the foregoing quotations, that the principle of contradiction is abrogated in emptiness. In some passages of the Sutra the identity of contradictory opposites is explicitly stated, and no attempt is made to mitigate the paradoxical character of this assertion.

95.

Sariputra : For what reason should a Bodhisattva be known as not lacking in perfect wisdom ?

Subhuti : Form is lacking in the own-being of form. And so for all things.

Sariputra : What, then, is the own-being of form, etc. ?

Subhuti : Non-positivity is the own-being of form, etc. It is in this sense that form is lacking in the own-being of form. And so with the other skandhas. Moreover, form, etc., is lacking in the mark which is characteristic of form, etc. The mark, again, is lacking in the own-being of a mark. The own-being, again, is lacking in the mark of being own-being.

Sariputra : A Bodhisattva who trains himself in this method, will he go forth to the knowledge of all modes ?

Subhuti : He will. Because all dharmas are unborn and do not go forth.

Sariputra : For what reason are all dharmas unborn, and do not go forth ?

Subhuti : Form is empty of the own-being of form. And so are all other dharmas. With regard to them no birth or going forth can be apprehended. It is thus that a Bodhisattva who practises perfect wisdom comes near to the knowledge of all modes.

96.

Subhuti : The Bodhisattva, the great being who practises perfect wisdom, should come to know of a thought which is even and exalted but he should not put his mind to it. For that thought is non-thought, since thought, in its essential, original nature is a state of transparent luminosity.

Sariputra : What is the transparent luminosity of thought ?

Subhuti : Thought which is neither conjoined with passion, nor disjoined from it ; which is neither conjoined with, nor disjoined from, hate, confusion, obsessions, coverings, unwholesome tendencies, fetters or what makes for views. That is the transparent luminosity of thought.

Sariputra : That thought which is non-thought, is that something which is ?

Subhuti : Can one find, or apprehend, in this state of absence of thought either a "there is" or a "there is not" ?

Sariputra : No, not that.

Subhuti : Was it then a suitable question when the Venerable Sariputra asked whether that thought which is non-thought is something which is ?

Sariputra : What then is this non-thoughthood ?

Subhuti : It is without modification or discrimination, it is the true nature of Dharma.

Sariputra : Are, like non-thoughthood, also form and the other skandhas without modification and discrimination ?

Subhuti : In the same way also form, and all the rest, are without modification and discrimination.

97.

The Lord : "Beings, beings", O Subhuti, as non-beings have they been taught by the Tathagata. Therefore are they called "beings". It is because of this that the Tathagata teaches, "Without self are all dharmas, without a living soul, without manhood, without personality".

98.

Sariputra : Of what is the term "Buddha" a synonym ?
Mañjusri : Of what, then, is the term "self" a synonym ?
Sariputra : "Non-production" is a synonym for "self".
Mañjusri : So it is, Sariputra. And that of which "self" is a synonym, of that also "Buddha" is a synonym. Or, the Track-less is another word for "Buddha". For a "Buddha" cannot easily be intimated by words. One who wants, Sariputra, to seek for the Tathagata, should seek for the self. For "self" and "Buddha" are synonymous. Just as the self does, absolute-ly, not exist and cannot be apprehended, just so the Buddha. As the self cannot be expressed by any dharma, so also the Buddha. The Buddha is the same as speechless silence.

99.

Mañjusri : "One who has not risen above fear", that, Sariputra, is a synonym for an Arhat whose outflows have dried up.
Sariputra : In what hidden senses, Mañjusri, do you say that ?
Mañjusri : He has no fears even about the least thing. What then will he rise above ?
Sariputra : What is the meaning of the phrase, "one who patiently accepts that which fails to be produced" ?
Mañjusri : It is a condition through which not even the least dharma has been produced.
Sariputra : What is the meaning of the term, "an undisciplined monk" ?
Mañjusri : "An undisciplined monk" means "an Arhat whose outflows have dried up". For it is the non-discipline which has been disciplined, and not the discipline.

100.

The Lord : Is there a synonym for "enlightenment ?"

Mañjusri : "The five deadly sins", that is a synonym for "enlightenment". For those five deadly sins have just the same essential original nature as enlightenment, because they do not exist. Therefore enlightenment has the essential nature of the deadly sins. It fully knows the deadly sins. But it is not a development which makes all dharmas cognizable. For all dharmas are absolutely uncognizable ; they are not seen, not cognized, not known by anyone.

C. THE BUDDHA

I. PERFECT WISDOM IS THE MOTHER OF THE BUDDHAS

101.

The Lord : If a mother with many children fell ill, the children would all exert themselves to prevent their mother from dying, to keep her alive as long as possible, to keep pain and unpleasantness away from her. Because they are aware that to her they owe their existence, that in great pain she has brought them into the world, that she has instructed them in the ways of the world. They would therefore look after her, give her everything that can make her happy, protect her well, make much of her, and they will hope that she be free from pain of any kind. In this way those sons honour their mother by giving her all that can make her happy, make much of her, cherish and protect her, because they are aware that she is their mother and begetter, that, in great pain she brought them into the world, that she instructed them in the ways of the world.

In just the same way the Tathagatas bring this perfection of wisdom to mind, and it is through their might, sustaining power and grace that people write, learn, study, spread and repeat it. And also the Tathagatas who dwell in other world systems just now,—for the weal and happiness of the many, out of pity for the many, for the weal and happiness of a great body of people, from pity for Gods, men and all beings,—they also all bring this perfection of wisdom to mind, and they put forth zeal so that this perfection of wisdom may last long, so that it may not be destroyed, so that Mara and his host may not prevent this perfection of wisdom from being taught, written, and practised. So fond are the Tathagatas of this perfection of wisdom, so much do they cherish and protect it. For she is their mother and begetter, she showed them this all-knowledge, she instructed them in the ways of the world. From her have the Tathagatas come forth. For she has begotten and shown that cognition of the all-knowing, she has shown them the world for what it really is. The all-knowledge of the Tathagatas has come forth from her. All the Tathagatas, past, future and present, win full enlightenment thanks to this perfection of wisdom. It is in this sense that the perfection of wisdom generates the Tathagatas, and instructs them in this world.

102.

The Lord : All the Tathagatas owe their enlightenment to just this perfection of wisdom,—whether they live in the past, future or present.   I also, Kausika, just now a Tathagata, owe my enlightenment to just this perfection of wisdom.

Sakra : A great perfection is this perfection of wisdom. For it allows the Tathagata to rightly know and to behold the thoughts and doings of all beings.

103.

Sakra : I pay homage, O Lord, to the perfection of wisdom. One pays homage to the cognition of the all-knowing when one pays homage to the perfection of wisdom.

The Lord : So it is.   For from it has come forth the all-knowledge of the Buddhas, the Lords, and, conversely, the perfection of wisdom is brought about as something that has come forth from the cognition of the all-knowing.   That is why one should course, stand, progress, and make efforts in this perfection of wisdom.

104.

The Lord : Therefore, Ananda, remember that it would be a serious offence against me if, after you had learned the Perfection of Wisdom, you should again forget it, cast it away, and allow it to be forgotten, and that would greatly displease me.   For the Tathagata has said that "the perfection of wisdom is the mother, the creator, the genetrix of the past, future and present Tathagatas, their nurse to all-knowledge".   Therefore then, Ananda, do I entrust and transmit to you this Perfection of Wisdom, so that it might not disappear.   One should learn it, and in so doing one should carefully analyse it grammatically, letter by letter, syllable by syllable, word by word.   For as the Dharma-body of the past, future and present Tathagatas this dharma-text is authoritative.

II.   DEFINITION OF A "BUDDHA"

A "Buddha" can be defined by an enumeration of his attributes.

They are in the main fivefold : the ten powers, the four grounds of self-confidence, the four analytical knowledges, the eighteen special Buddha-dharmas (105), *and omniscience,* (106, 107).

105.

The Lord : What are the ten powers of a Tathagata ? Here, Subhuti, a Bodhisattva who courses in the perfection of wisdom (1) wisely knows, as it really is, what can be as what can be, and what cannot be as what cannot be. (2) He wisely knows, as they really are, the karmic results of past, future and present actions and undertakings of actions, as to place and cause. (3) He wisely knows, as they really are, the various elements in the world. (4) He wisely knows, as they really are, the various dispositions of other beings and persons. (5) He wisely knows, as they really are, the higher and lower faculties of other beings and persons. (6) He wisely knows, as it really is, the Way that leads everywhere. (7) He wisely knows, as they really are, the defilement, purification and origination of all trances, deliverances, concentrations and meditational attainments. (8) He recollects his various previous lives. (9) With his heavenly eye he knows the decease and rebirth of beings as it really is. (10) Through the extinction of the outflows, he dwells in the attainment of that emancipation of his heart and wisdom, which is without outflows, and which he has, in this very life, well known and realised by himself. He wisely knows that "Birth is exhausted for me ; the higher spiritual life has been lived. I have done what had to be done. After this becoming there will be none further". And all that without any apprehension whatever.

What are the four grounds of self-confidence ? (1) That I who claim to be fully enlightened am not fully enlightened in those dharmas,—I see nothing to indicate that anyone, be he recluse, or Brahmin, or God, or Mara, or Brahma, or anyone else in the whole world, can with justice make this charge. And as I do see nothing to indicate this, I dwell in the attainment of security, of fearlessness, of self-confidence. I claim my exalted place as leader of the herd. I rightly roar the lion's roar in the assembly, and set rolling the sacred wheel which can not be set rolling by any recluse or Brahmin or God or Mara or Brahma, or anyone else in the world, with justice. (2) That I, who claim to have dried up the outflows, have not completely dried

them up, that is impossible.   I see nothing to indicate, etc., as
(1).   (3) That those dharmas which I have described as impediments should have no power to impede him who pursues them,
that is impossible.   I see nothing to indicate, etc., as (1).
(4) That he who progresses on what I have described as the Path,
leading to the holy going forth, leading to penetration, leading
to the right extinction of ill for him who does so, should not
go forth to the right extinction of ill, that is impossible.   I see
nothing to indicate etc., as (1).   And all that without any
apprehension whatever.

What are the four analytical knowledges ?   They are the
analytical knowledge of the meaning, of the dharma, of speech,
of inspired speech.   And they also should be practised without
any apprehension whatever.

What are the eighteen special dharmas of a Buddha ?
From the night when the Tathagata knew full enlightenment,
to the day when he becomes extinct in Nirvana, during all this
time, the Tathagata 1. Does not stumble, 2. He is not rash or
noisy in his speech. 3. He is never deprived of his mindfulness.
4. He has no perception of difference, 5. His thought is never
unconcentrated, 6. His evenmindedness is not due to lack of
consideration, 7. His zeal never fails, 8. His vigour never fails,
9. His mindfulness never fails, 10. His concentration never fails,
11. His wisdom never fails, 12. His deliverance never fails,
13. All the deeds of his body are preceded by cognition, and
continue to conform to cognition, 14. All the deeds of his
voice are preceded by cognition, and continue to conform to
cognition, 15. All the deeds of his mind are preceded by cognition, and continue to conform to cognition, 16. His cognition
and vision regarding the past period of time proceeds unobstructed and freely. 17. His cognition and vision regarding
the future period of time proceeds unobstructed and freely,
18. His cognition and vision regarding the present period of
time proceeds unobstructed and freely.

106.

The Lord : A Tathagata's knowledge of all modes is the
undoubting cognition of all dharmas in all their aspects and
in all the three times.   A Bodhisattva's knowledge of the
path is his going forth on the Buddha-vehicle, in full knowledge
of the Paths of all three vehicles, but not satisfied with the

vehicles of the Disciples and Pratyekabuddhas. "All-know-ledge", finally, is the certain cognition of the absence of an individual self in whatever is found in the twelve sense-fields, and it is known to the Disciples and Pratyekabuddhas.

107.

The Lord : As many beings as there are in countless world systems of them I know, in my wisdom, the manifold trends of thought. And why ? "Trends of thought, trends of thought", Subhuti, as no-trends have they been taught by the Tathagata. Therefore are they called "trends of thought". And why ? A past thought cannot be apprehended ; a future thought cannot be apprehended ; a present thought cannot be appre-hended.

III. THE BUDDHA'S PHYSICAL BODY AND HIS DHARMA-BODY

108.

The Lord : Those who by my form did see me,
And those who followed me by my voice,
Wrong the efforts they engaged in,
Me those people will not see.
From the Dharma should one see the Buddha,
For the Dharma-bodies are the guides.
Yet Dharmahood is not something one should
become aware of,
Nor can one be made aware of it.

109.

Sakra : It is because the Lord has trained himself in just this perfection of wisdom that the Tathagata has acquired and known full enlightenment or all-knowledge.

The Lord : Therefore the Tathagata does not derive his name from the fact that he has acquired this physical personal-ity, but from the fact that he has acquired all-knowledge. And this all-knowledge of the Tathagata has come forth from the perfection of wisdom. The physical personality of the Tathagata, on the other hand, is the result of the skill in means of the perfection of wisdom. And that becomes a sure founda-tion for the acquisition of the cognition of the all-knowing by others. Supported by this foundation the revelation of the cognition of the all-knowing takes place, the revelation of the Buddha-body, of the Dharma-body, of the Samgha-body.

110.

Sakra : In a true sense this perfection of wisdom is the body of the Tathagatas. As the Lord has said : "The Dharmabodies are the Buddhas, the Lords. But, monks, you should not think that this individual body is my body. Monks, you should see me from the accomplishment of the Dharma-body !" But that Tathagata-body should be seen as brought about by the reality-limit, i.e. by the perfection of wisdom.

111.

Dharmodgata : A man, scorched by the heat of the summer, during the last month of summer, at noon, might see a mirage floating along, and might run towards it, and think : "There I shall find water, there I shall find something to drink". What do you think, son of good family, has that water come from anywhere, or does that water go anywhere, to the Eastern great ocean, or the Southern, or the Western or the Northern ?

Sadāprarudita : No water exists in that mirage. How could its coming or going be conceived ? That man again is foolish and stupid if, on seeing the mirage, he forms the idea of water where there is no water. Water in its own-being certainly does not exist in that mirage.

Dharmodgata : Equally foolish are all those who adhere to the Tathagata through form and sound, and who in consequence imagine the coming or going of a Tathagata. For a Tathagata cannot be seen from his form-body. The Dharmabodies are the Tathagatas.

112.

The Lord : What do you think, Subhuti, can the Tathagata be seen by the possession of his marks ?

Subhuti : No indeed, Lord. For what has been taught by the Tathagata as the possession of marks, that is truly a no-possession of no-marks.

The Lord : Wherever there is a possession of marks, there is fraud. Wherever there is a no-possession of no-marks, there is no fraud. Hence the Tathagata is to be seen from no-marks as marks.

113.

The Lord : What do you think, Subhuti, should the Tathagata be seen by means of the thirty-two marks of the Superman ? Subhuti : No, indeed, Lord. Because those thirty-two marks of the Superman which were taught by the Tathagata, as no-marks have they been taught by the Tathagata. Therefore are they called the "thirty-two marks of the Superman".

114.

Dharmodgata : The perfect body of the Buddhas and Lords is dependent on causes and conditions, and it has been brought to perfection through exertions which have led to many wholesome roots. But the augmenting of the Buddha-body does not result from one single cause, nor from one single condition, nor from one single wholesome root. And it is also not without cause. It has been co-produced by a totality of many causes and conditions, but it does not come from anywhere. And when the totality of causes and conditions has ceased to be, then it does not go to anywhere. It is thus that you should view the coming and going of the Tathagatas, and that you should conform to the true nature of all dharmas. And it is just because you will wisely know that the Tathagatas, and also all dharmas, are neither produced nor stopped, that you shall become fixed on full enlightenment, and that you shall definitely course in the perfection of wisdom and in skill in means.

115.

The Lord : How does a Bodhisattva develop the recollection of the Buddha ? He does not attend to the Tathagata through form, or feeling, etc. For form, feeling, etc., have no own-being. And what has no own-being, that is non-existent. The recollection of the Buddhas through non-attention to form, etc., is a non-attention, a non-recollection. A Tathagata further should not be attended to through the thirty-two marks of a Superman, nor should he be attended to as golden-bodied, nor should he be attended to through the effulgence of his halo, or through the eighty minor characteristics. And that for the same reasons as before. A Tathagata should, further, not be attended to through the mass of his morality or the mass of his concentration, or the mass of his wisdom, or the mass of his emancipation, or the mass of his vision and cognition of emancipation. And that for the same reasons as before. A Tathagata should, further, not be attended to through the ten powers of a Tathagata, or the four grounds of self-confidence, or the four analytical knowledges, or the great compassion, or the great friendliness, or the eighteen special Buddha-dharmas. For all these have no own-being, and what has no own-being that is non-existent. A non-recollection is therefore the recollection of the Buddha.

IV. ENLIGHTENMENT

116.

Subhuti : One speaks of "enlightenment". Of what is that a synonym ?

The Lord : "Enlightenment", that is a synonym of emptiness, of Suchness, of the reality-limit, of the realm of Dharma. Moreover "enlightenment" is Suchness, without falsehood, unaltered Suchness, unaltered non-existence ; therefore is it called "enlightenment". Moreover "enlightenment" is a mere word, therefore is it called "enlightenment". Moreover "enlightenment" means an undifferentiated object. It belongs to the Buddhas, the Lords; therefore is it called "enlightenment". The Buddhas, the Lords, have fully known it ; therefore is it called "enlightenment".

117.

Subhuti : How can the Lord say that full enlightenment is hard to win, exceedingly hard to win, when there is no one who can win enlightenment ? For, owing to the emptiness of all dharmas, no dharma exists that would be able to win enlightenment. All dharmas are empty. That dharma also, for the forsaking of which Dharma is demonstrated, that dharma does not exist. And also that dharma which would be enlightened in full enlightenment, and that which should be enlightened, and that which would cognize (the enlightenment), and that which should cognize it,—all these dharmas are empty. In this manner I am inclined to think that full enlightenment is easy to win, not hard to win.

The Lord : Because it cannot possibly come about, is full enlightenment hard to win, because in reality it is not there, because it cannot be discriminated, because it has not been fabricated as a false appearance.

Sariputra : Also because it is empty is it hard to win, Subhuti. For it does not occur to space that it will win full enlightenment. As such, i.e. as without own-being, should these dharmas be known in enlightenment. For all dharmas are the same as space.

118.

Mañjusri : Enlightenment is not discerned by anyone, nor is it fully known, nor seen, nor heard, nor remembered. It is neither produced nor stopped, neither described nor expounded. Insofar as there is, Sariputra, any enlightenment, that enlightenment is neither existence nor non-existence. For there is nothing that could be fully known by enlightenment, nor does enlightenment fully know enlightenment.

Sariputra: Has the Lord, then, not fully known the realm of Dharma ?

Mañjusri : The Lord has not fully known the realm of Dharma. For the realm of Dharma is just the Lord. If, Sariputra, the realm of Dharma were something that had been fully known by the Lord, then the realm of non-production could be stopped. But the realm of Dharma is just the same as enlightenment. For the realm of Dharma is devoid of existence. "Non-existent are all dharmas", that is a synonym of enlightenment, and it is thus that the realm of Dharma comes to be called thus. For, as the domain of the Buddha, all dharmas are non-separateness.

119.

Subhuti : Is then, O Lord, enlightenment attained through an unproduced dharma ?

The Lord : No, Subhuti.

Subhuti : Is then enlightenment attained through a produced dharma ?

The Lord : No, Subhuti.

Subhuti : Is then enlightenment attained neither through a produced, nor through an unproduced path ?

The Lord : No, Subhuti.

Subhuti : How then is enlightenment attained ?

The Lord : Enlightenment is attained neither through a path nor through a no-path. Just the path is enlightenment, just enlightenment is the path.

Subhuti : If that is so, then a Bodhisattva has already attained enlightenment. How then is it that a Tathagata is recognized by the thirty-two marks of a superman, the ten powers, the four grounds of self-confidence, the four analytical knowledges, the eighteen special Buddha-dharmas ?

The Lord : What do you think, Subhuti, does a Buddha attain enlightenment ?

Subhuti : No, Lord. A Buddha does not attain enlightenment. Just the Buddha is enlightenment, just enlightenment is the Buddha.

120.

The Lord : What do you think, Subhuti, is there any dharma which has been fully known by the Tathagata as "the utmost right and perfect enlightenment", or is there any dharma which has been demonstrated by the Tathagata ?

Subhuti : No, not as far as I understand the Lord's teaching. For this dharma which has been fully known or demonstrated by the Tathagata, that should not be seized upon, that should not be talked about, and it is neither dharma nor no-dharma. And why ? Because an Absolute exalts the Holy Persons.

V.   THE TATHAGATA AND THE BUDDHA-DHARMAS

The Lord : Whoever says that the Tathagata goes or comes, or stands or sits, or lies down, he does not understand the meaning of my teaching. And why ? "Tathagata" is called one who has not gone to anywhere, and who has not come from anywhere. Therefore is he called "the Tathagata, the Arhat, the fully Enlightened One".

122.

The Lord : How, Manjusri, should the Tathagata be seen and honoured ?

Manjusri : Through the mode of Suchness (tathatā) do I see the Tathagata, through the mode of non-discrimination, in the manner of non-observation. I see him through the mode of non-production and non-existence. But Suchness does not attain full knowledge,—thus I see the Tathagata. Suchness does not become, does not cease to become,—thus do I see the Tathagata. Suchness does not stand at any point or spot,—

thus do I see the Tathagata. Suchness is not past, future or present,—thus do I see the Tathagata. Suchness is neither brought about by duality nor by non-duality,—thus do I see the Tathagata. Suchness is neither defiled nor purified,—thus do I see the Tathagata. Suchness is neither produced nor stopped,—thus do I see the Tathagata. In this way the Tathagata is seen and honoured.

123.

The Lord : Do you, Mañjusri, reflect on the Buddhadharmas?

Mañjusri : No indeed, Lord. If I could see the specific accomplishment of Buddhadharmas, then I would reflect on the Buddhadharmas. But the development of perfect wisdom is not set up through discriminating any dharma, and saying, "these are the dharmas of ordinary people, these are the dharmas of Disciples, these are the dharmas of Pratyeka-buddhas, these are the dharmas of fully enlightened Buddhas". The son of good family who has given himself up to the Yoga of the development of perfect wisdom does just not apprehend that dharma which would allow him to describe these dharmas as dharmas of ordinary people, or as dharmas of those in training, or as dharmas of the adepts, or as dharmas of fully enlightened Buddhas. Because as absolutely non-existent I do not review those dharmas. Such a development, O Lord is a development of perfect wisdom . . . Perfect wisdom, when developed, is not a donor of the Buddhadharmas, nor a destroyer of the dharmas of an ordinary person. Just that, O Lord, is the development of perfect wisdom, where there is neither the stopping of the dharmas of an ordinary person, nor an acquisition of the Buddhadharmas.

124.

The Lord : There is not any dharma through which the Tathagata has known full enlightenment. And that dharma which has by the Tathagata been fully known and demonstrated, on account of that there is neither truth nor fraud. Therefore the Tathagata teaches, "all dharmas are the Buddha's own and special dharmas". And why ? "All dharmas", O Subhuti, have as no-dharmas been taught by the Tathagata. Therefore all dharmas are called "the Buddha's own and special dharmas".

SUPPLEMENT

THE MANTRIC PATH

We now come to a side of the Prajñāpāramitā teaching which seems strange and incredible to modern ears : It is the belief that the teachings of the Sutra can be condensed into words of magical power, either Mantras or Dharanis. This belief seems to have been held from quite early times onwards, although, of course, in the Tantric age of Buddhism, after A.D. 600, it received increased emphasis. It is in this case almost impossible to dissociate the teaching from its linguistic expression, and much of the force of the original is lost in translation. Both historical accuracy, and, to some extent, the needs of meditation, forbid, however, a complete suppression of this aspect of the doctrine.

125.

The Lord : The sons or daughters of good family, who will take up this deep perfection of wisdom, will bear it in mind, recite, study, and repeat it, and attend to it wisely, even if they should, while repeating this deep perfection of wisdom, go into the midst of a battle, they will come out of it uninjured and unharmed. It is impossible, and it cannot be, that the life of that son or daughter of good family should be checked who, while repeating this perfection of wisdom, has gone into battle. That is impossible. Any spear or arrow that someone might aim at them cannot touch their bodies. And why ? Because that son or daughter of good family have for a long, long time well practised the six perfections. They have vanquished the spears and arrows of their own greed, hate and delusion, and the spears and arrows of the greed, hate and delusion of others they have also learnt to vanquish. Based on this perfection of wisdom one should develop this perfection of wisdom. Such a one will also not be lacking in the thought of all-knowledge, And why ? A lore of great magical power (mahā-vidyā) is this perfection of wisdom, a lore of utmost power, a lore of un-equalled power. The son or daughter of good family, who are trained in this lore, they do not set their hearts on disturbing their own peace, nor that of others. For one who is trained therein perceives nowhere a self, nor a living soul, nor a creature, nor a person, nor a personality, nor a man, nor one who acts, nor one who feels, nor one who generates, nor one who sees. Thus unperceiving, he does no harm to himself or to others.

126.

Sakra : Which are the advantages that one can expect from perfect wisdom here and now ?

The Lord : The devotees of perfect wisdom will not die an untimely death, nor from poison, sword, fire, water, staff, or violence. When they bring to mind and repeat this perfection of wisdom, the calamities which threaten them from kings and princes, from king's counsellors and king's ministers, will not take place. If kings, etc., would try to harm those who again and again bring to mind and repeat the perfection of wisdom, they will not succeed. Because the perfection of wisdom upholds them. Although kings, etc., may approach them with harmful intent, they will instead decide to greet them, to converse with them, to be polite and friendly to them. For this perfection of wisdom entails an attitude of friendliness and compassion towards all beings. Therefore, even though the devotees of perfect wisdom may be in the middle of a wilderness infested with venomous vipers, neither men nor ghosts can harm them, except as a punishment for past deeds.

Thereupon one hundred Wanderers of other sects approached the Lord with hostile intent. Sakra, Chief of Gods, perceived those Wanderers from afar, and he reflected : "Surely, those Wanderers of other sects are approaching the Lord with hostile intent. Let me then recall as much of this perfection of wisdom as I have learned from the Lord, let me bring to mind, repeat and spread it, so that those Wanderers cannot approach the Lord, and the preaching of this perfection of wisdom may not be interrupted".

Thereupon Sakra, Chief of Gods, recalled as much of this perfection of wisdom as he had learned from the Lord, brought it to mind, repeated and spread it. Those Wanderers of other sects thereupon reverently saluted the Lord from afar, and went off on their way.

Thereupon it occurred to the Venerable Sariputra : "For what reason have those heretical Wanderers reverently saluted the Lord from afar, and have departed on their way ?"

The Lord : When Sakra, Chief of Gods, perceived the

thoughts of those hostile Wanderers of other sects, he recalled
this perfection of wisdom, brought it to mind, repeated and
spread it, with the object of turning back those Wanderers of
other sects who wanted to quarrel, dispute and obstruct, and of
preventing them from approaching the place where the perfection of wisdom is being taught. And I have granted per-
mission to Indra, Chief of Gods. Because I saw not even one
single pure dharma in those Wanderers. They all wanted to
approach with hostile intent, with thoughts of enmity.

Thereupon it occurred to Mara, the Evil One : "The four
assemblies of the Tathagata are assembled, and seated face
to face with the Tathagata. Face to face with the Tathagata
those Gods of the realm of sense-desire and of the realm of
form are sure to be predicted in that assembly as Bodhisattvas
to full enlightenment. Let me now approach to blind them".
Thereupon Mara conjured up an army, and moved towards
the place where the Lord was. Thereupon it occurred to
Sakra, Chief of Gods : "Surely, this is Mara, the Evil One,
who, having conjured up an army, moves towards the place
where the Lord is. This is not the array of King Bimbisara's
army, or of King Prasenajit's army, or of the army of the
Sakyas, or of the Licchavins. For a long time Mara the Evil
One has pursued the Lord, looking for a chance to enter,
searching for a chance to enter, intent on hurting beings. I will
now recall thiṣ perfection of wisdom, bring it to mind, repeat
and spread it". Thereupon Sakra recalled just this perfection
of wisdom, brought it to mind, repeated and spread it. Im-
mediately Mara, the Evil One, turned back again, and went
on his way.

127.

The Lord : The doors of the dharanis, Subhuti, belong to
the great vehicle of the Bodhisattva, the great being. Which
are they ?

The syllable A is a door to the insight that all dharmas are
unproduced from the very beginning (ādy-anutpannatvād).
The syllable RA is a door to the insight that all dirt (rajas) has
vanished from all dharmas. The syllable PA is a door to the
insight that all dharmas have been expounded in the ultimate
sense (paramārtha). The syllable CA is a door to the insight
that one cannot apprehend the decease (cyavana) or rebirth of

any dharma, because all dharmas do not decease, are not reborn. The syllable NA is a door to the insight that the Names of all dharmas have vanished ; and the essential nature of names is neither apprehended nor destroyed.

The syllable LA indicates that all dharmas have escaped from the world (loka) ; because the causes and conditions of the creeping plant (latā) of craving have been utterly destroyed. The syllable DA is a door to all dharmas from having circumscribed "tamed" and "taming" (dānta-damatha). The syllable BA indicates that the Bonds of all dharmas have departed. The syllable *D*A indicates that the tumult (*d*amara) of all dharmas has vanished. The syllable SHA indicates that one apprehends no attachment (sha*n*ga) to any dharma ; one is neither attached nor bound.

The syllable VA is a door to all dharmas because the sound of the paths of speech (vākpatha-ghosha) has been quite cut off. The syllable TA is a door to all dharmas because Suchness (tathatā) does not waver. The syllable YA is a door to all dharmas because of the non-apprehension of that which is in accordance with truth (yathāvad). The syllable SH*T*A is a door to all dharmas because of the non-apprehension of a support (sh*t*ambha). The syllable KA is a door to all dharmas, because of the non-apprehension of an agent (kāraka).

The syllable SA is a door to all dharmas because of the non-apprehension of sameness (samatā) ; it also means that one does not completely (samantād) depart. The syllable MA is a door to all dharmas, because of the non-apprehension of mine-making (mamakāra). The syllable GA is a door to all dharmas because of the non-apprehension of motion (gamana). The syllable STHA is a door to all dharmas because of the non-apprehension of rest (sthāna). The syllable JA is a door to all dharmas, because of the non-apprehension of birth (jāti).

The syllable *S*VA is a door to all dharmas because of the non-apprehension of a principle of life (*s*vāsa). The syllable DHA is a door to all dharmas, because of the non-apprehension of the realm of Dharma (dharma-dhātu). The syllable *S*A is a door to all dharmas, because of the non-apprehension of calming-down (*s*amatha). The syllable KHA is a door to all dharmas, because of the non-apprehension of the sameness of empty space (kha). The syllable KSHA is a door to all dharmas, because of the non-apprehension of extinction (kshaya).

I

The syllable STA is a door to all dharmas, because each dharma is fixed (stabdha ?) in its place, and never leaves it. The syllable J*N*A is a door to all dharmas, because cognition (jñāna) cannot be apprehended. The syllable RTHA is a door to all dharmas, because an object (artha) cannot be apprehended. The syllable HA is a door to all dharmas, because one cannot apprehend a root-cause (hetu). The syllable BHA is a door to all dharmas, because of the non-apprehension of breaking-up (bha*n*ga).

The syllable CHA is a door to all dharmas, because of the non-apprehension of cutting-off (chedana). The syllable SMA is a door to all dharmas, because of the non-apprehension of remembrance (smara*n*a). The syllable HVA is a door to all dharmas, because of the non-apprehension of true appellations (āhvāna). The syllable TSA is a door to all dharmas, because of the non-apprehension of will-power (utsāha). The syllable GHA is a door to all dharmas, because (things and persons) are not apprehended as one solid mass (ghana) each.

The syllable *T*HA is a door to all dharmas, because of the non-apprehension of fabricated appearances (vi*t*hāpana). The syllable *N*A is a door to all dharmas, because strife (ra*n*a) has departed. The syllable PHA is a door to all dharmas, because no fruit (phala) is apprehended. The syllable SKA is a door to all dharmas because the Skandhas are not apprehended. The syllable YSA is a door to all dharmas because of the non-apprehension of decay (ysara=jarā).

The syllable *S*CA is a door to all dharmas, because of the non-apprehension of good conduct (cara*n*a). The syllable *T*A is a door to all dharmas, because of the non-apprehension of the other shore (*t*alo ?). The syllable *D*HA is a door to all dharmas because of the non-apprehension of unsteadiness (iñjana ?). In their ultimate and final (nish*t*hā=ni*d*ha ?) station dharmas neither decease nor are they reborn.

No syllables are in conventional use except those just mentioned.

128.

The Lord said to the holy Lord Avalokita, the Bodhisattva, the great being : For a long time you have been engaged in furthering the weal of all beings, their welfare, their happiness, and their instruction. Therefore then, son of good family, listen and attend well. I will teach you the Perfection of Wisdom in a Few Words, which has great merit : When they merely hear it, all beings will extinguish the obstacles which arise from their past deeds, and they will definitely end up in enlightenment. And the Mantras of those beings who labour zealously at the evocation of Mantras will succeed without fail . . .

Thereupon the Lord at that time taught the Perfection of wisdom as follows :

The Bodhisattva, the great being, should have an even mind, he should have a friendly mind towards all beings, he should be thankful, he should be grateful, he should desist in his mind from all evil. And this Heart of Perfect Wisdom should be repeatedly recited, "Homage to the Triple Jewel! Homage to Sākyamuni, the Tathagata, the Arhat, the fully Enlightened One ! i.e. Om ! O the Sage ! O the Sage ! Homage to the great Sage ! All Hail !" Through having gained this Perfection of Wisdom have I reached full enlightenment, and from it all the Buddhas have come into being. I also have heard this very Perfection of Wisdom from Mahāsākyamuni, the Tathagata. Therefore then, in front of all the Bodhisattvas you have been predicted to Buddhahood, with the words : "You, O young man, will become in a future period a Tathagata called Samantarasmi Srikutarājā, an Arhat, a fully Enlightened One, perfect in knowledge and conduct, a Sugata, World-knower, unsurpassed, leader of men to be tamed, Teacher of Gods and men, a Buddha, a Lord". And all those who will hear this name, will bear it in mind, recite it, write it, and explain it in detail to others, and who, when this has been made into a written book, will preserve and worship it, they will, even through learning just this little bit, become Tathagatas. I.e. "Om ! May I conquer, may I conquer ! You who are in the likeness of a lotus ! Intimate, intimate ! O You, the path for going along ! Possessor of wisdom, possessor of wisdom ! Goddess ! Protectress ! You who rescue us from strife, who ward off the hostile actions of others ! Fulfil, fulfil, Lovely Lady, the hopes of all ! Clean away all my karma-coverings, and those of all beings ! You who are sustained by the Buddhas ! All Hail !" This, O son of good family, is the Perfection of Wisdom in the ultimate sense, the genetrix of all the Buddhas, the mother of the Bodhisattvas, giver of enlightenment, remover of all evil. Even all the Buddhas are unable to express in words her advantages, even after hundreds of kotis of kalpas. Where it is merely being recited, there all the Assemblies are consecrated, and all the mantras are realised face to face.

Thereupon the holy Avalokitesvara, the Bodhisattva, the great being said to the Lord : For what reason, O Lord, is this the Perfection of Wisdom in a Few Words ?

The Lord said : Because it is an easy means. If there are beings who are dull and stupefied, if they will but bear in mind this Perfection of Wisdom in a Few Words, will recite it, read it, cause it to be read, they will all, through this easy means, end up in enlightenment. For this reason, son of good family, has this Perfection of Wisdom been compressed into a Few Words.

The holy Avalokitesvara, the Bodhisattva, the great being, then said to the Lord : It is wonderful, O Lord, it is greatly wonderful, O Sugata, how, O Lord, for the weal of all beings this discourse on dharma has been pronounced, for the sake of dull people, for their welfare, for their happiness.

129.

One should also repeatedly and mindfully recall the following Mantra : "Homage, homage to the Perfection of Wisdom, the lovely, the holy, who is adorable and endowed with infinite virtues ! Homage also to the knowledge of all modes of all the Tathagatas, and to all Buddhas and Bodhisattvas ! i.e. Om, O Wisdom, O Wisdom ! O Great Wisdom ! O Wisdom, the Illuminator ! Wisdom, the Giver of Light ! Remover of ignorance ! Success, Good Success, Help me Succeed ! Blessed Lady ! Beautiful in all your limbs ! Loving Mother ! Your hand is held out to me ! Give courage ! Stand, stand ! Tremble, Tremble ! Shake, Shake ! Yell, Yell ! Go, Go ! Come, Come ! Blessed Lady ! Do not delay your coming ! All Hail !"

When someone has taken up this perfection of wisdom, he will thereby bear in mind the Perfection of Wisdom in 100,000 Lines. He should always murmur it. All the obstacles (arising) from (his past) deeds will then be extinguished. Deceased from here he will be reborn as one who is mindful, self-possessed and of matchless wisdom. He will bear in mind of all the Tathagatas of the three times all the dharmas without exception, and he will have taken hold of all the mantras and spells. Deceased from here he will be reborn as one who is mindful, self-possessed and of great wisdom.

130.

The Lord : Ananda, do receive, for the sake of the weal and happiness of all beings, this perfection of wisdom in one letter, i.e. A.

LIST OF PASSAGES QUOTED

SURVEY

This Survey correlates the *numbers* of the extracts in this work (indicated in *italics*) with the editions and manuscripts of the Prajñāpāramitā texts from which they are derived. These are quoted by giving the chapter in Roman numerals, followed by the pages of the edition, or the folios of the manuscript. The following sources have been used :

Satasāhasrikā : ed. P. Ghosha, 1902-1913. Only ch. I-XII. After ch. XIII the manuscripts Cambridge Add. 1633, 1630, 1627,1632
Pañcaviṁśatisāhasrikā : ed. N. Dutt 1934. Only part I. Later passages from the manuscript Cambridge Add. 1628.
Ashṭādaśasāhasrikā : Manuscript Stein ch. 0079a, and Tibetan Kanjur, 3 vols.
Daśasāhasrikā : Tibetan Kanjur, 1 vol.
Ashṭasāhasrikā : ed. R. Mitra 1888.
Suvikrāntavikrāmīparipṛicchā : ch. I ed. T. Matsumoto, Die Prajñāpāramitā Literatur, 1932.—ch. II ed. T. Matsumoto, in P. Kahle, Studien, 1935.
Saptaśatikā : First part (quoted by pages) ed. J. Masuda, Journal of the Taisho University, vol. 6-7, 1930.—Second part (quoted by folios) : ed G. Tucci, Memorie della R. Acad. dei Lincei, vol. 17, 1923.
Vajracchedikā : ed. M. Mueller, 1881.
Svalpāksharā : Manuscript As. Soc. Bengal 107578.
Hṛidaya : ed. E. Conze, Journal of the Royal Asiatic Society, 1948.
Ashṭaśataka : Tibetan Kanjur, Sna tshogs, 250a-252a.
Kauśika : Manuscript Stein 0044.
Ekāksharī : Tibetan Kanjur, Sna tshogs, 255b-256a.

Satasāhasrikā : I 118-119 : *85.* iii 495-502 : *96.* ix 1446-1450 : *105.* 1450-2 : *127.* x 1460 : *44, 45.* 1461 : *11.* 1466-9 : *55.* 1469-70 : *14.* xviii f. 130 : *125.* xlv f. 119 : *66.* LIII f. 279-283 : *91.* LVIII ? : *49.*
Pancaviṁśatisāhasrikā : page 18 : *41.* 35-37 : *23.* 40-1 : *6.* 78 : *61.* 89-90 : *73.* 90 : *89.* 99-100 : *60.* 114-5 : *72.* 136-8 : *95.* 153-4 : *88.* 169-70 : *12.* 175-6 : *47.* 182 : *48.* 192-4 : *67.* 194-5 : *40.* 196-8 : *82.* 245, 254 : *65.* 255-6 : *90.* 259-62 : *70.* 263 : *77.* 263-4 : *42.* 266 : *50.* folio 500-501 : *92.* 505-506 : *115.*
Ashṭādaśasāhasrikā : LXV f. 611 : *116.* LXXIV : *83.* LXXVII f. 707 : *119.*
Daśasāhasrikā ii : *106.*
Ashtasāhasrikā i 5 : *53.* 12-13 : *74.* 20-21 : *87.* ii 34-8 : *78.* 38-40 :

PUBLISHER'S NOTE

The following is a complete list of the twenty major works of the Prajñāpāramitā literature, as translated by Dr. Conze, and available in typescript at the prices given. All enquiries should be addressed to the publishers.

TEXTS

1. The Large Perfection of Wisdom. E: With divisions of no. 21. 150,000: £5/-/-. Part I. E : 70,000 : 25/-.
2. The Perfection of Wisdom in 8,000 Lines. E : 110,000 : 30/-.
3. The Perfection of Wisdom in 2,500 Lines. Chapters 1—2 : S : 10/- ; E : 9,000 : 5/-. Chapters 3—6 : T : 20/-.
4. Ratnaguṇasaṃcayagāthā. S : 15/-. T : 15/-. E : 17,000 : 10/-.
5. The Perfection of Wisdom in 700 Lines. S : 12/6 ; E : 13,500 : 7/6.
6. Diamond Sutra. S : 10/- ; E : 7,000 : 5/-.
7. The Perfection of Wisdom in 150 Lines. S : 10/- ; T : 10/- ; E : 5,000 : 7/6.
8. The Perfection of Wisdom in 50 Lines. T : 3/- ; E : 1,200 : 2/-.
9. The Perfection of Wisdom in a Few Words. S : 2/6 ; T : 2/6 ; E : 1,000 : 2/-.
10. The 108 Names of Perfect Wisdom. (S : 2/6) ; T : 2/6 ; E : 1,000 : 2/-.
11. The Perfection of Wisdom for Kauśika. S : 2/6 ; T : 2/6 ; E : 700 : 2/-.
12. The Perfection of Wisdom for Suryagarbha. T : 2/6 ; E : 600 : 1/-.
13. The 25 Doors to Perfect Wisdom. T : 2/6 ; E : 500 : 1/-.
14. The Perfection of Wisdom for Candragrabha. T : 2/6 ; E : 500 : 1/-.
15. The Heart of Perfect Wisdom. S : 2/6 ; T : 2/6 ; (E in BT).
16. The Perfection of Wisdom for Vajraketu. T : 2/6 ; E: 300: 1/-.
17. The Perfection of Wisdom for Samantabhadra. T : 2/6 ; E : 250 : 1/-.
18. The Perfection of Wisdom for Vajrapāni. T : 2/6 ; E : 250: 1/-.
19. The Perfection of Wisdom in One Letter. T : 1/- ; E : 150: 1/-.
20. Rahulabhadra. Prajñāpāramitāstotra. S : 2/6. (E : in BT).

COMMENTARIES

21. Abhisamayālaṅkāra. S : 10/-. (E : Rome 1954, 35/-).
22. Literary History of the Prajñāpāramitā. 50,000 : £2/-/-.

23. Dictionary of the Prajñāpāramitā Texts. 9,000 sanskrit terms, with references, and all the English, and many Tibetan, equivalents £5/-/-.
24. Introduction to Part I of the Large Prajñāpāramitā. 15,000 : 20/-.
25. Short Commentary to the Hridaya. 6,000 : 10/-.
26. Long Commentary to the Hridaya. 40,000 : 30/-.
27. Ninno. Summary based on de Visser, etc. E : 7,000 : 5/-.
28. Tibetan-sanskrit Dictionary, 9,000 Tibetan words. £2 10/-.

S=Sanskrit
T=Tibetan
E=English, followed by the number of words.
BT="Buddhist Texts".